Chaim Potok

Twayne's United States Authors Series

Warren French, Editor

Indiana University, Indianapolis

TUSAS 503

CHAIM POTOK
(1929-   )

Chaim Potok

By Edward A. Abramson

University of Hull

Twayne Publishers
A Division of G.K. Hall & Co. • Boston

Chaim Potok

Edward A. Abramson

Copyright © 1986 by G.K. Hall & Co.
All Rights Reserved
Published by Twayne Publishers
A Division of G.K. Hall & Co.
70 Lincoln Street
Boston, Massachusetts 02111

Copyediting supervised by Lewis DeSimone
Book production by Elizabeth Todesco
Book design by Barbara Anderson

Typeset in 11 pt. Garamond
by Modern Graphics, Inc., Weymouth, Massachusetts

Printed on permanent/durable acid-free paper
and bound in the United States of America

Library of Congress Cataloging in Publication Data

Abramson, Edward A.
  Chaim Potok.

  (Twayne's United States authors series; TUSAS 503)
  Bibliography: p. 150
  Includes index.
  1. Potok, Chaim—Criticism and interpretation.
I. Title. II. Series.
PS3566.069Z54 1986   813'.54   86-3139
ISBN 0-8057-7463-7

*I am grateful to my wife, Nikki,
for her understanding and patience*

Contents

About the Author

Edward Abramson was born in New York City, grew up and went to school there, and received his B.A. degree from the City University of New York. He received his M.A. from the University of Iowa, then taught as an instructor in the English Department of East Carolina University, in North Carolina. He journeyed to England to do research for his doctorate and was awarded the Ph.D. degree in English literature from the University of Manchester. Since 1971 he has been assistant lecturer, then lecturer, in American literature in the Department of American Studies at the University of Hull.

He has published many articles and reviews on literary subjects. His study of American writing, entitled *The Immigrant Experience in American Literature,* was published in 1982 by the British Association for American Studies.

Preface

This is the first full-length study of Chaim Potok's writing, my intention being to show that he has now reached a stage in his literary career when he must be taken seriously as an author. As a Jewish-American writer, a label that Potok dislikes, he belongs to that group of authors whose Jewish consciousness makes itself manifest in the form of particular Jewish characters or concerns or, perhaps more frequently, certain themes and tonal qualities that often show a somewhat different orientation to the world than that found in the work of non-Jewish American writers. However, Potok's concerns often differ markedly from even those of Jewish-American authors in that he places a great deal of stress upon Judaism as a religious force. Most Jewish-American authors, while having perhaps some concern with strictly religious aspects of Judaism, do not place a great deal of emphasis upon it, being more concerned with cultural and social aspects of Jewishness to which the religion often contributes but need not be a central factor.

Potok's protagonists suffer difficulties for reasons that are different from those that cause problems for the protagonists of both Jewish and non-Jewish American authors. While characters in twentieth-century novels often suffer from problems of alienation and, not infrequently, identity crises, they do not often have to contend with the requirements of an ancient and demanding faith and a tightly knit religious community. Potok's protagonists do, and this aspect of their lives takes on a role as part of the central conflict in each novel. That his novels have been best-sellers requires some explanation given the rather esoteric nature of his subject matter and its seeming divergence from the mainstream of twentieth-century American literature.

This study, consisting of a close analysis of Potok's major fiction and nonfiction, will show the development of his skill and the complexity of his themes. Judgments by critics will be evaluated, as will Potok's treatment of certain recurrent themes such as religion in conflict with society, individual needs in conflict with institutional beliefs, tradition versus the modern, and fathers and sons. In addition, there will be an elucidation of the importance of specific Jewish beliefs and rituals to Potok's work.

I am very much indebted to Chaim Potok for his willingness to answer questions and provide biographical and bibliographical details. I am also grateful to David Chessman, a doctoral candidate in American literature at the University of Hull, for his stimulating ideas and assistance in compiling lists of critical source material. My thanks also goes to the staff of the Brynmor-Jones Library (Inter-Library Loan Section) of the University of Hull for their efforts in tracing material from occasionally obscure sources in various parts of the world. Any shortcomings in judgment or interpretation remain my own.

Edward A. Abramson

University of Hull
Kingston upon Hull
England

Chronology

1929   Herman Harold (Chaim Tzvi in Hebrew) born in the Bronx, New York. Father a Belzer Hasid; mother a descendant of the great Hasidic Ryzhyner dynasty. Attends orthodox Jewish parochial schools.

1939   Shows talent in drawing and painting; dissuaded by father and Talmud teachers from seriously pursuing art.

1945   Reads *Brideshead Revisited* by Evelyn Waugh; decides to become a writer.

1949   Nonfiction and fiction published in college year book; becomes literary editor of the year book.

1950   B.A. in English literature from Yeshiva University, summa cum laude. Leaves Jewish orthodox fundamentalism.

1954   Graduates from the Jewish Theological Seminary of America as a Conservative rabbi; Bible prize, Hebrew Literature Prize, Homiletics Prize. Becomes national director of the Leaders Training Fellowship, a nationwide youth organization of the Conservative movement.

1955   Becomes a chaplain in the United States Army; serves in Korea with a front line medical battalion and a combat engineer battalion. Begins his first novel.

1957   Teaches at the University of Judaism in Los Angeles. Becomes director of Camp Ramah in California, a year-round educational camp under the auspices of the Conservative movement.

1958   Marries Adena Mosevitzky, a psychiatric social worker.

1959   Moves to Philadelphia; enters the Graduate School of the University of Pennsylvania. Becomes scholar-in-residence at Har Zion Temple in Philadelphia. Completes first novel about Korea, repeatedly rejected by publishers as not commercial. Begins second novel.

1962   Daughter Rena born.

1963   Spends year in Israel completing Ph.D. dissertation, "The

Rationalism and Skepticism of Solomon Maimon," under the name Herman Harold Potok. Writes first draft of second novel.

1964   Moves with family to Brooklyn, New York. Becomes managing editor of *Conservative Judaism*. Joins the faculty of the Teachers' Institute of the Jewish Theological Seminary. Writes a series of pamphlets on ethics for the Leaders Training Fellowship.

1965   Daughter Naama born. Receives Ph.D. in philosophy from the University of Pennsylvania. Becomes associate editor of the Jewish Publication Society of America.

1966   Becomes editor in chief of the Jewish Publication Society. Completes revision of second novel. Appointed to the Jewish Publication Society Bible Translation Committee.

1967   *The Chosen;* nominated for National Book Award; receives Edward Lewis Wallant Prize.

1968   Son Akiva born.

1969   *The Promise;* receives Athenaeum Award.

1972   *My Name Is Asher Lev.*

1973   Goes to Israel to live with family; settles in Jerusalem.

1974   Becomes special projects editor of the Jewish Publication Society.

1975   *In the Beginning.*

1977   Returns to the United States from Israel; settles in Pennsylvania.

1978   *Wanderings: Chaim Potok's History of the Jews.*

1981   *The Book of Lights.*

1982   *The Chosen* appears as a major film.

1983   Teaches philosophy of literature at the University of Pennsylvania as a visiting professor in the Department of Philosophy.

1985   *Davita's Harp* and *Ethical Living for a Modern World: Jewish Insights,* a collection of pamphlets.

Chapter One
From Rabbi to Writer

Chaim Potok grew up in the Bronx in an Orthodox Jewish family. He accepted his Judaism happily but discovered a larger world with different values that often conflicted with his strict Jewish beliefs. This conflict, which Potok has referred to as a "culture confrontation," was of central importance in his development as a writer. He has written of this experience:

I had little quarrel with my Jewish world. I was deep inside it, with a child's slowly increasing awareness of his own culture's richness and short-comings. But beyond the tiny Hannibal of our apartment, there was an echoing world that I longed to embrace; it streamed in upon me, its books, movies, music, appealing not only to the mind but also to the senses. Faintly redolent of potential corruptions of the flesh, dark with the specter of conquest by assimilation, it seemed to hold out at the same time the promise of worldly wisdom, of tolerance, of reward for merit and achievement, and—the most precious promise of all—the creations of the great minds of man. . . .[1]

Much of the literature created by Jewish-American writers came out of the conflicts between older cultural and religious values and those of secular America. With Potok these conflicts are heightened and made very specific because of his protagonists' commitment to a religious viewpoint. Potok's personal conflicts, his attraction-repulsion toward the secular American society, can be seen clearly in his writing. He desired neither to isolate himself totally within the Orthodox religious community in which he had been raised, nor to assimilate completely into what he refers to as the "paganism" of secular American society. It is this choice, this dilemma, that his protagonists most frequently confront: a "core-to-core confrontation" between their own Jewish subculture and aspects of an attractive "umbrella culture." He feels that this confrontation creates—at it did in himself and does in his protagonists—a "between-person" who can achieve positive insights into more than one culture

1

but may well pay the price of feeling at home totally in no single one.

In 1954 Potok was ordained a Conservative rabbi. The Conservative movement in America holds a position between the Orthodox fundamentalists on the one hand and the Reform and more liberal movements on the other. While attempting to preserve much of traditional Jewish practice and belief, Conservatism allows its adherents more room for interpretation of Jewish tradition as well as more freedom to apply the findings of secular scholarship to religious matters. This type of Judaism permitted Potok to retain his ties to traditionalism while opening up the world of secular humanistic writing to him. This was essential because of his critical intelligence. He has written that because of his exposure to the sciences and symbolic logic, he found a need "to forge a religious life out of what I call provisional absolutes. . . . I must constantly be prepared to alter my basic religious assumptions should the need arise."[2] Like Danny Saunders in *The Chosen*, who became a psychologist but retained his practice of Judaism nonetheless; or Reuven Malter, in the same novel, who was most adept at mathematics but became a rabbi, so Potok needed a foot in both the secular and religious worlds.

For him the need of freedom of choice in religious terms was even more pressing than for Danny or Reuven, as can be seen by the above comment and his remark that "A ritual act which is not charged with meaning, which does not qualitatively enhance my existence, is drained of value and cannot become part of my acting-out pattern of religious behaviour. . . . The criterion of selectivity is my own inner being, my own awareness of the fundamental principles underlying Jewish law, but the selection is always made— and this is a vital point—from a base of knowledge and not out of ignorance or for reasons of personal convenience.[3] Neither of the two aforementioned characters, both being varying degrees of Orthodox, would permit themselves quite as much latitude with Jewish tradition.

Potok describes the crisis through which he lived when he was "suspended in a theological void. . . ." He retained his Jewish practices while trying to create a type of Judaism that would permit him to encompass the new secular knowledge which so attracted him. Paradoxically, it was just this new knowledge that made it possible for him to achieve a reconciliation with Judaism: "The problems that troubled me then have been resolved by the very disciplines—modern historiography and the scientific approach to the sacred texts of Judaism which others regard as an open threat to religion. . . . They give the sources a form, a focus, a vitality which is impossible within a fundamentalist stance. They have made Judaism come alive for me. . . ."[4] Potok pursued the problems related to scientific text criticism and Bible scholarship in both *The Promise* and *In the Beginning;* the roots of his concern with these problems lay in his own life experiences.

Potok's third novel, *My Name Is Asher Lev,* also has roots in his past. From childhood he was interested in painting. He relates how one summer his parochial school "inexplicably" hired an artist to give a course in painting to the children: "He watched me move colors across a canvas board one day and took me aside. 'How old are you, kid?' he asked. 'Who've you studied with?' That was my first step into the world of western art. In my childhood, what Joyce was to Jesuits, painting was to Talmud."[5] So, at the age of ten Potok began to discover an aesthetic side to his nature that bore little relation to the mind-centred world of the Talmud. Painting and photography became increasingly important to him. Whereas Asher Lev had to make the agonizing choice between abandoning his art or his Hasidic community, Potok was able to remain attached to the style of Judaism that appealed to him and, in addition, pursue his interest in the visual arts. Asher probably will retain aspects of his Jewish practices, but his Brooklyn community is dead to him.

Potok served for fifteen months as a chaplain in Korea and Japan. He had written his first novel about his experiences there, but it was never published. In his fifth novel, however, he returned to the Orient and created in *The Book of Lights* one of his most complex works. Steeped in the Jewish mysticism of the Kabbalah and full of moral decisions fraught with anguish, it marks a new departure for him in the sense that he is solely involved with the adult world. Continuity exists in that he is still concerned with questions of moral choice coming out of conflicts between the "umbrella civilization" and Judaism. His experiences, however, were of a very different sort than those that underpinned the previous novels. With its lack of awareness of Judaism, the Orient—and the atomic age which Western culture brought so tragically to it—provided the basis for a novel dense with apocalyptic overtones. Potok's experiences in the Far East exposed him to moral and social issues that had to await the development of his literary skill in order to find expression.

The growth of his interest in literature and in trying to become a writer can be traced to his teenage years. He faced the same problem which Nathaniel Hawthorne relates in the Custom House sketch in *The Scarlet Letter,* that is, the tradition out of which both men came did not respect secular literature. Hawthorne's narrator relates how his Puritan ancestors would be appalled at what he became (the narrator may be viewed as probably a thinly disguised spokesman for Hawthorne himself)—"A writer of storybooks!" That sort of vocation, he thinks, would not seem to them a suitable method of glorifying God or serving mankind. In Chaim Potok's Jewish tradition, "writing stories occupies no point of any significance in the hierarchy of values by which one measures achievement. Scholarship—especially Talmudic scholarship—is the measure of an individual. Fiction . . . is at best a frivolity, at worst a menace."[6]

This attitude of the tradition meant that Potok had to become a rebel in order to pursue an interest in serious fiction. In his third novel, he examined the plight of a boy who faced perhaps an even greater problem: how to develop his aesthetic sense through painting, an art form even further removed than fiction from the Jewish tradition. Asher Lev had to leave his Hasidic community; Chaim Potok, as we have seen, was able to remain closely attached to the Jewish tradition through a more modern interpretation of it than was permitted Asher Lev.

Potok recalls the first time that he became aware of the immense attraction of fiction:

When I was about fourteen or fifteen years old, I read *Brideshead Revisited* by Evelyn Waugh. That was the first serious adult novel I ever read. . . . I was overwhelmed by that book. Somehow Evelyn Waugh reached across the chasm that separated my tight New York Jewish world from that of the upper-class British Catholics in his book. . . .

From that time on, I not only read works of literature for enjoyment but also studied them with Talmudic intensity in order to teach myself how to create worlds out of words on paper. . . .

In time I discovered that I had entered a tradition—modern literature. Fundamental to that tradition was a certain way of thinking the world; and basic to that was the binocular vision of the iconoclast. . . .[7]

If it is valid to say that a great deal of literary art depends upon the author's convincingly treating various conflicts, one can see clearly from what sources Potok's art derives its force. As a rabbi, he studied the Talmud and appreciated the profundity of the commentators; as a fiction writer, he had to accept a different orientation to the world that would not have met with the approbation of the Talmudic commentators.

His early admiration of *Brideshead Revisited,* in particular Waugh's ability to communicate the essence of the narrow social and religious world of upper-class British Catholics, exposed Potok to the possibilities of communicating his own narrow world through fiction. In order to communicate this world, he had, paradoxically, to move away from a narrow orientation and become not an apologist for it but, so far as possible, an "objective" observer and presenter. The "binocular vision" that he refers to as "basic" caused him to see various aspects of traditional Judaism in as critical a manner as Waugh had seen certain aspects of Roman Catholicism. While his iconoclasm certainly had its limits, Potok did not demur from showing which areas of Judaism he preferred and which he found wanting.

As Waugh affected him in a broad sense, so Potok has pointed to those authors whom he feels influenced him most in terms of style. He has written that "The sonnets of Milton taught me my regard for simplicity and careful naming; the flattening effect I learned from Stephen Crane."[8] He has also said that he admires Ernest Hemingway's style and James Joyce's treatment of religious themes. As this study proceeds, we shall see the ways in which Potok's style develops in relation to his novels. Suffice it to say at this point that he has been much criticized for both a "simplicity" of style and for the "flattening" effect that has failed to impress many critics, who have seen in it not an example of Mies van der Rohe's dictum that "Less is more," but merely a situation showing that "Less is less." While this criticism has some validity, it is not entirely fair but is common enough to demand the detailed consideration that it shall receive throughout this study.

Potok has written a number of short stories and sees them linked to his novels and essays by many themes: "First, there is an ongoing attempt to deal bluntly with dark realities beneath seemingly smooth surfaces: racial bigotry in 'Reflections on A Bronx Street'; Holocaust memories in 'The Dark Place Inside'; anti-Semitism in 'Miracles for

a Broken Planet'; the horrors of war in 'The Fallen'; Zionism in 'A
Tale of Two Soldiers'—to cite only a few of the themes."[9] He points
out that these and other themes occur repeatedly in his novels but
that stylistically the stories are very different from the novels, being
"more compressed, laconic, and elliptical . . .; the stories—in
particular, "The Dark Place Inside"—are more *my* voice and are
closer to the third-person narrative style in *The Book of Lights* than
to the first-person novels like *The Chosen,* where a careful balance
had to be effected between the narrator's unsophisticated literary
voice and the requirements of literary style."[10] His favorite story is,
quite rightly, "The Dark Place Inside." It is written in concise
language that is highly implicative and carries the tension of the
piece well. However, these stories, set in America and Israel, cannot
really prepare one for Potok's major work. To see what he is capable
of creating, one must turn to the novels themselves.

Chapter Two
The Chosen
The Hasidim and the Orthodox

Many non-Jews think that the Jewish community is a homogeneous one with each member having substantially the same beliefs as the other. While there is less sectarianism among Jews than Christians, there is a wide divergence in the interpretation of law and ritual among Liberal, Reform, Conservative, Orthodox, and Hasidic Jews. Hasidic Jews are the most extreme in their beliefs, feeling that they adhere to the only correct form of Judaism and by so doing are fulfilling God's will.

Hasidism arose in eighteenth-century Poland as a reaction against the formal learning and intellectuality stressed by the rabbinic Judaism of the time. This learning was largely restricted to discussion and study of the Talmud, a collection of sixty-three books usually set out in eighteen folio volumes. The Talmud consists of civil, religious, and ethical laws based upon Jewish teaching and biblical interpretation that was originally oral and was passed down over the ages from Israel's earliest history. Around 200 C.E., Rabbi Judah the Prince collated them into the *Mishnah*. Scholars studied the *Mishnah* closely, their discussions being printed as the *Gemara*. The Talmud is the *Mishnah* and *Gemara* together. There are two Talmuds, one produced in Palestine and one in Babylon at each of the two great academies. The Palestinian Talmud was never completed, so the one usually studied and considered more authoritative is the Babylonian Talmud, finished about 500 C.E. It is the greatest work of Jewish religious literature after the Bible itself and has had a profound effect upon Jewish life and thought.

The difficulty of the Talmud meant that it was accessible to only a very small number of individuals who would often keep themselves aloof from the mass of the people. It was in this situation that Israel Baal Shem began to preach that the way to serve God was not through scholarship, study, and learning but through piety, love, and prayer. The Baal Shem (literally "Master of the Name") also

7

stressed joy and emotion in worship, even through the use of song and dance. He was a charismatic individual, and many who were skeptical of his practices were won over. Eventually this included almost half of the Jews in Eastern Europe, who referred to him as the "Baal Shem Tov," the "Master of the Good Name" in recognition of his saintly nature.

The established religious authorities counted themselves as *Mitnagdim* (opponents) and were determined to destroy the new movement which they saw as heretical. They did not succeed, but great bitterness grew between the two groups, which is reflected in Potok's first novel, *The Chosen,* where Reb Saunders, his son Danny, and the Hasidic sect to which they belong are compared in terms of their attitudes toward things religious and secular with David Malter, his son Reuven, and the Orthodox group that holds their loyalties. Unlike the Vilna Gaon, the eighteenth-century leader of the *Mitnagadim,* David Malter is somewhat more compassionate and understanding of Reb Saunder's position, since he appreciates that "the fanaticism of men like Reb Saunders kept us alive for two thousand years of exile. If the Jews of Palestine have an ounce of that same fanaticism and use it wisely, we will soon have a Jewish state."[1]

In spite of this understanding which David Malter shows, when he hears that Reb Saunders's is raising Danny in silence his reaction is closer to that of the eighteenth-century opponent: "He sat up straight on the bed, his body quivering. 'Hasidim!' I heard him mutter, almost contemptuously. 'Why must they feel the burden of the world is only on their shoulders?' " (266). This viewpoint is shared by the Orthodox Jews in the synagogue where he prays with his son.

This distaste with Hasidism is based upon their self-righteousness; the enclosed nature of their communities; what is often seen as the dry scholasticism of their methods of studying the Talmud, especially surprising since their beginnings were rooted in a rebellion against this very scholasticism; the anti-Zionism of the Williamsburg Hasidim; and, perhaps most importantly, the position and role of the *tzaddik* within their communities.

Louis Jacobs has written:

Hasidism is hardly intelligible without the doctrine of the *Zaddik,* the spiritual superman whose holy living not only provides his followers with inspiration for their lives but who raises them aloft with him through the spiritual powers that are his. . . .

The central idea in this connection is that the *Zaddik's* prayer on behalf of his followers can achieve results far beyond the scope of their own puny efforts at prayer. . . . God has delivered into his hands the means whereby the flow of divine grace can either be arrested or encouraged to flow. All depends on the *Zaddik*.[2]

The reaction of non-Hasids to this set of beliefs is that they border on idolatry and have no place in true Jewish belief. Jews are supposed to approach God directly, intermediaries not being required. A rabbi is someone who knows more about Jewish law than a layman, but a rabbi is not necessary in order for religious services to be held. Any Jew who can gather a *minyan* (ten Jewish males) may conduct a religious service. Indeed, a Jewish proverb states that "Nine rabbis do not make a minyan, but ten cobblers do." In other words, the overwhelming centrality which the Hasidim give to their rabbis is not shared by most non-Hasidic Jews.

Potok presents this conflict in *The Chosen*. Reuven Malter is astonished at the manner in which Reb Saunders is treated by his followers, particularly when Danny tells him that his entire community uprooted from Russia and traveled to America because Reb Saunders said that they should go. They followed him, Danny says, because "He's a *tzaddik*." To Reuven, however, this explanation is not sufficient:

"I can't understand how Jews can follow another human being so blindly."
"He's not just another human being."
"Is he like God?"
"Something like that. He's a kind of messenger of God, a bridge between his followers and God."
"I don't understand it. It almost sounds like Catholicism." (122)

This virtual deification of Reb Saunders extends to Danny, who is expected to inherit his father's office and is assumed also to have taken on the mantle of his sanctity. Thus, an aged Hasid with a white beard touches Danny's arm reverently, a gesture that Reuven finds most distasteful. As an Orthodox Jew, Reuven believes that he is following the 613 commandments set out for Jews as best he can. Hasidism appears to be an anachronism, and one with some highly questionable features.

As with most fanatical religious groups, the Hasidim are firmly convinced that their way of approaching God is right and all other ways are wrong. There is, however, a further level of belief among Hasids. They believe that their rebbe is right, has the only entirely true way of performing the various rituals, and places proper emphasis upon different aspects of the faith. Each rebbe stresses slightly different aspects of Judaism: certain prayers may be stressed instead of others; different interpretations of Jewish law may occur; the length of various services may be different; the attitude toward other Jews and non-Jews will vary from one rebbe to another and, therefore, extend to his followers. The results of these Hasidic beliefs are depicted throughout *The Chosen,* particularly in relation to conflicts between Hasidic and Orthodox Jewish beliefs.

The dramatic beginning to the novel turns a baseball game into a holy war. Reuven states that his school is looked down upon because it is filled with pupils who are interested in getting away from the ghetto mentality that pervades other Brooklyn Jewish schools. The Hasidim consider observant Jews like Reuven little better than heathen, and Danny threatens to "kill you *apikorsim*":

The word had meant, originally, a Jew educated in Judaism who denied basic tenets of his faith, like the existence of God, the revelation, the resurrection of the dead. To people like Reb Saunders, it also meant any educated Jew who might be reading, say, Darwin, and who was not wearing side curls and fringes outside his trousers. I was an *apikoros* to Danny Saunders, despite my belief in God and Torah, because I did not have side curls and was attending a parochial school where too many English subjects were offered and where Jewish subjects were taught in Hebrew instead of Yiddish, both unheard-of-sins. . . . (30–31)

The Hasidim have suffered even more than other Jews because of their purposeful visibility; that is, they have throughout their history worn their Jewish identity before the world. During the Nazi era in Europe, they suffered savage persecution. After the war, those rebbes who survived gathered together those of their people who remained and took them to America or what was then Palestine to try to reestablish their communities. They tried to move their culture intact from one continent to another and to preserve it in the face of strong assimilatory pressures. Whereas many Orthodox and other Jews were concerned to blend as much as possible into American society, the Hasidim enclosed themselves in their own communities and did not suffer problems of whether or not it was desirable to become a part of the new country. Thus, in one sense, they had an easier time in America than less "enlightened" Jews: they knew precisely who they were and what values they wanted to retain. In their community in the Williamsburg section of Brooklyn, which is where *The Chosen* is set, Hasidim who originated largely from Hungary, but also from Poland, set up tightly organized groups. As Solomon Poll points out: "Thus among the Hasidim of Williamsburg are the most outspoken separatists. By isolating themselves, they try to (a) re-create a traditional society that they have transplanted from Europe, (b) divert threats of assimilation by the secular world outside, and (c) combat internal change."[3]

Hasidim outside Williamsburg are usually much more open to outsiders. Indeed, the Habad-Lubavitch, located in the Crown Heights section of Brooklyn; the Bostoner, located in Boston; and the Bratslaver Hasidim, located in various parts of New York City as well as in Jerusalem, all seek converts to their type of Hasidism from their fellow Jews. The Satmar Hasidim, who are the largest group in Williamsburg, are probably the ones on which Potok modeled Reb Saunders and his Hasidim. Their extremism provided Potok with a strong dramatic contrast to the more broad-minded Orthodoxy of David Malter although, as mentioned, members of his synagogue dislike the Hasidim almost as much as the Hasidim dislike them. As with Reb Saunders's group, the Satmar are anti-Zionist, and Potok uses the struggle to create a Jewish state as an important dramatic conflict in the novel.

Solomon Poll explains the basis of the conflict: "Whereas some Hasidim are strong Zionists and see in the State of Israel a sign of the coming of the Messiah, the Hasidim of Williamsburg are anti-Zionist. They reject everything and everyone that is associated with the new state. They conceive that the existence of the State of Israel is a threat to their traditional perception of the Messiah, because 'all of it must emerge through holiness.' "[4] This belief in the Messiah has been with the Jews throughout most of their long history. In the darkest days of persecution, the belief that redemption would surely come helped the people survive their tribulations. The Messiah was seen as a man of flesh and blood, not a supernatural being and certainly not divine. It is this individual whom the Hasidim of Williamsburg, and Reb Saunders in *The Chosen,* await to usher in an era of holiness and peace. In addition, the Messiah is to be responsible for gathering together the people of Israel from all the nations of their exile in order to bring them to a reconstituted Holy Land.

For many Orthodox Jews, like David Malter, a somewhat different but no less valid Messianic belief exists; that is, a belief in a Messianic Age. This belief existed alongside that of a Messianic individual in the writings of the prophets and certain Jewish sages and stressed not that a single man would hold the Messianic key but that through the work of good men the "Days of the Messiah" could be brought into existence. This concept stressed the efforts of individuals here and now to work in order to bring about, with God's help, a redeemed mankind on earth and a reborn Israel. Belief in a Messianic Individual or in a Messianic Age need not be exclusive. Both beliefs lead to the same ends for mankind and for Israel; both require divine guidance. The only difference lies in the number of individuals affected by the divine will and working toward the same Godly ends.

The response to Zionism in *The Chosen* is related to differing attitudes toward Messianism, God's will, and the Holocaust. Reb Saunders's response to the murder of six million Jews is to say that it is God's will; it is a seemingly passive acceptance of the catastrophe. David Malter's response is to say that American Jews, now constituting the largest Jewish community in the world, must work to give the tragedy meaning through preserving the Jewish people. His approach is an obviously active one that finds expression in Zionism: "Some Jews say we should wait for God to send the Messiah. We cannot wait for God! We must make our own Messiah! We must rebuild American Jewry! And Palestine must become a Jewish homeland!" (197).

Reb Saunders's "passive" approach is only apparently so in that he accepts what he believes to be God's will. He is, however, most active in his resistance to the efforts of people who believe as David Malter does, which belief he sees as antithetical to this will. When Reuven mentions to him that many people now believe that the time has come for a Jewish homeland to be established in Palestine, he explodes: "God will build the land, not Ben Gurion and his goyim! When the Messiah comes, we will have Eretz Yisroel, a Holy Land, not a land contaminated by Jewish goyim!" (198). Allen Guttman comments that "The thought that David Ben Gurion can be considered a Gentile may amuse some readers, but Reb Saunders speaks from the same tradition that burned the works of Moses Maimonides and excommunicated Baruch Spinoza."[5] Even Danny sees the wrongheadedness of his father's approach to this issue, when he disclaims the belief for himself (he would join a Zionist group if not for his father) but tells Reuven with a certain wryness: " 'Herzel didn't wear a caftan and side curls,' Danny said. 'Neither does Ben Gurion' " (199).

The result of this difference of opinion is that Reb Saunders almost destroys Reuven's and Danny's friendship by refusing to let Danny speak to Reuven, and ostracizing (Reuven uses the word "excommunicate") both Reuven and his father from the Saunders's family. Reb Saunders emerges from the novel as a fanatical patriarch who rules his family and flock with an iron hand. However, Potok clearly does not want the reader to detest Reb Saunders but to appreciate the immense pressures under which he labors. Even Danny holds him in great respect and awe, and at times he emerges as a wise, compassionate man who carries on his shoulders the weight of suffering of his Hasidim and of the world. When Reuven lashes out at his seeming heartlessness in raising Danny in silence, his father, who has borne the brunt of Reb Saunders's wrath over Israel, tells him, "I did not have to raise you that way. I am not a *tzaddik*" (282).

The great detail with which Potok presents Hasidic life in Williamsburg leaves the reader impressed with the veracity of the author's observations. Although a novel need not be "true" in the sense of history or sociology, *The Chosen* clearly has the ring of truth in terms of factualness. How surprising it is then to come upon a critic who questions some of the aspects of Potok's depiction of Hasidic life. Judah Stampfer writes of *The Chosen* that "at the time of its action, I visited almost every Yeshiva in the United States, as well as half of its Hasidic *rebbes,* some of whose dynastic sons were my close personal friends. . . . Whatever Potok's personal experience, the book is a valuable rendition of Yeshiva life, and this constitutes its greatest asset. Its description of American Hasidic life, as I have known it, has only the most superficial resemblance to its outer behavior."[6]

Stampfer proceeds to list his disagreements with Potok's description of Hasidic life in America: he has never seen a Talmudic debate in public on the Sabbath such as takes place between Reb Saunders and Danny, and states that no Hasidic rebbe would deliberately

14 CHAIM POTOK

make errors with holy writ; there is too much stress on learning, Hasidic rebbes preaching holiness and faith, not close textual analysis; Hasidic women are not as docile as Potok presents Danny's sister, wooing being necessary if the daughter is to accept the parents' choice of husband and rejection of the proposed groom a distinct possibility; it is not likely that Danny would be out for blood, as in the baseball game, as this is a sin; the one to inherit the rebbe's position is decided afresh in each case according to the man involved, Danny's having a younger brother eliminating any real tension from the issue.[7]

The conclusion that Stampfer draws is that "Read as a conflict between the Hasid and the *Misnagdim,* the book is too freighted with anti-Hasidic prejudice to be of value. . . . But Potok's depiction of Yeshiva life has a ring of truth. The book should then be read as a book about the conflict between true piety and blind fanaticism, with the Hasidic element an emblem of the fanatic.[8] Even if Potok has used poetic license in order to heighten the dramatic effect of certain aspects of the plot, the novel remains true to the spirit of each group and to the divisions between them. Indeed, at the time of this writing, disagreements between Hasidic sects themselves have been appearing in American newspapers. The Satmar Hasidim have accused the proselytizing Lubavitch of attempting to take members away from them; the Lubavitch accuse Satmar members of being responsible for a number of attacks on them, including throwing rocks and beating two Lubavitcher rabbis before cutting off their beards. Battles between Hasidim and the secular authorities in Israel are well known. In the light of the overt violence occurring between Hasidic sects themselves, Potok's descriptions of Hasidic rigidity and dislike of outsiders seems convincing, even if certain details may not be completely accurate. *The Chosen* is, after all, a novel and not a historical or sociological text.

Jewish and Non-Jewish Worlds

The Chosen is set largely within a Jewish world, the characters approaching and having to cope with their problems within almost self-contained Jewish communities. The novel opens with a dramatic baseball game between a fanatical Hasidic sect of Ultra-Orthodox Jews and a group of Orthodox Jews who follow the commandments but not the particular idiosyncrasies of the Hasids. It is here that we meet Danny Saunders, the son of the leader of the Hasidic sect and heir apparent to his father's post. Because of what we later learn to be pressure from his father not to engage in secular pursuits at all, Danny feels that his team must win, thus proving that they can beat "lesser" Jews at their own game, as it were. He turns the game into a holy war and, in batting a line drive at Reuven, almost blinds him in one eye.

Reuven is the son of the more liberal David Malter, who has been helping choose library books for Danny unbeknown to his father. Danny is a genius and is chafing at the highly restricted Hasidic world that prevents him from expanding his mind with secular reading, particularly psychology. Danny's father, Reb Saunders, has been raising him in silence in order to try to develop his soul since he will be inheriting his father's role as leader of the community. Reb Saunders wants to speak to Danny through Reuven, a process that David Malter understands and encourages. Unfortunately, a hiatus occurs between the two fathers on account of differing views toward the rebuilding of the State of Israel by secular Jews, and Reb Saunders refuses to allow Danny to speak to Reuven.

When Israel is proclaimed a Jewish state and Jewish boys begin dying to defend it, Reb Saunders's resistance begins to break down; he allows his son to speak to Reuven again, and the central plot concern of whether Danny will leave the community to become a psychologist reemerges. Danny does leave the community to study psychology and does not take on his inherited role; this passes to his younger brother. Reuven, perhaps ironically, becomes a rabbi. The story is a highly Jewish one but, as we shall see, the non-Jewish world and Jewish elements from outside the tightly knit communities within which the novel is set impinge upon the central characters with increasing force.

The only non-Jewish characters who appear in the novel are patients or relatives in the Jewish hospital to which Reuven goes for treatment of his injured eye. The most thoroughly presented is Tony Savo, who occupies the bed next to Reuven. Potok presents him as a decent man who has no anti-Jewish prejudice and who illustrates in a minor way the importance of faith. He has been a boxer, and will lose his eye because of punches received in the ring. He sees Reuven eating while wearing a skullcap and comments on the importance of religion. Then he says, "Could've been on top if that guy hadn't clopped me with that right the way he did. Flattened me for a month. Manager lost faith. Lousy manager" (49). A page later he repeats the point about his manager losing faith. While this remark may be interpreted as the manager "losing faith" in Tony Savo, we learn that Tony wanted to be a priest once but chose the ring instead, a "Lousy choice," he now feels. As these points are made against the background of the radio's reports of the fighting toward the end of World War II, one feels the contrast between the violence in Europe and simple faith. It is a somewhat simplistic comparison but does highlight Potok's feeling that violence implies a lack of faith both in mankind and in something greater than man.

Danny arrives and tries to apologize to Reuven, who will not listen to him. Mr. Savo comments:

> "He one of these real religious Jews?" Mr. Savo asked.
> "Yes."
> "I've seen them around. My manager has an uncle like that. Real religious guy. Fanatic. Never had anything to do with my manager though. Small loss. Some lousy manager." (67–68)

There is a dual implication here in that his manager's loss of faith is seen as being in some way responsible for Tony Savo's plight and the fact that his manager's religious uncle would have nothing to do with him is yet another sign of the manager's faithlessness. However, Danny and the uncle, religious though they are, are "cloppers": "You're a good kid. So I'm telling you, watch out for those fanatics. They're the worst cloppers around" (81). Religion is a good thing, but not the fanatical type of religion followed by the Hasidim; that is destructive. Thus, Potok uses a non-Jew to present the argument at the center of the religious confrontation which pervades the novel. Indeed, much later on when Reuven decides to become a rabbi, he remembers Tony Savo:

> "America needs rabbis," my father said.
> "Well, it's better than being a boxer," I told him.
> My father looked puzzled.
> "A bad joke," I said. (219)

The only other non-Jews who appear in the novel are Billy Merrit and, very briefly, his father. Billy's eye operation is unsuccessful, and he remains blind; Mr. Savo has to have one eye removed. Only

Reuven completely heals. Indeed, good fortune will follow him throughout the novel, everything he puts his hand to reaching a satisfactory conclusion. It is one of the criticisms which has been leveled at the novel: everything works out well for the protagonists, Potok being at base highly optimistic, at least as far as his main characters are concerned. This issue will be pursued further later in this chapter.

The world outside the Hasidic community has a crucial effect upon Danny Saunders, the central figure in the plot. He tells Reuven that he feels "trapped" by the assumption that he will carry on the generations-old tradition that his family provides the rebbe for the community. He finds study of the Talmud extremely limiting and must sneak off to the public library and seclude himself behind the shelves in order to read books from the secular world. It is noteworthy that "misbehavior" in *The Chosen* consists of a genius reading the writings of some of the best minds of the last two centuries; one is not dealing here with Danny's reading pornography or popular culture. The nature of his reading highlights the repressiveness of the Hasidic world that his father rules.

Danny points out that once he is rebbe he can read whatever he likes since so far as his people are concerned he can do no wrong. Interestingly, he would then also become a type of psychologist, albeit with an all-pervading religiosity. His people would come to him with their personal problems as well as with those relating directly to religious law. It would, however, be fatuous to see the role of rebbe as simply one of religious psychologist. He would have to be seen to be taking their suffering upon himself; hence Reb Saunders's attempts to develop in him a soul as well as a mind.

In Europe, in another century, the possibilities open to Danny in the secular world would have been far more limited than they are in America. He might have done what Solomon Maimon did in the eighteenth century in Poland; that is, go to Germany and immerse himself in studying the great philosophers and in writing philosophical texts. It is noteworthy here that the subject of Potok's doctoral dissertation was "The Rationalism and Skepticism of Solomon Maimon." Indeed, David Malter cites Maimon as a parallel to Danny. He says: "Reuven, Reb Saunders' son has a mind like Solomon Maimon's, perhaps even a greater mind. And Reb Saunders' son does not live in Poland. America is free. There are no walls here to hold back Jews. Is it so strange, then, that he is breaking his father's rules and reading forbidden books? he cannot help himself" (113).

Danny's attraction to psychology is an attraction to what has become almost a secular religion, with people like Sigmund Freud constituting members of a priestly caste. Not only does Danny discover that he can use the methods of Talmudic study in deciphering Freud's writings, but Reb Saunders finds that he can partially justify his son's choice of vocation in that Danny "will be a *tzaddik* for the world. And the world needs a *tzaddik*" (280). This explains Hugh Nissenson's remark that "Danny's conflict between the secular and the spiritual life has been daringly, and brilliantly resolved."[9] One might also add, given Reb Saunders's perhaps somewhat too easy acceptance of his son's choice, that the conflict has been a bit too comfortably resolved.

Part of the reason for Danny's being drawn to the secular world lies in the comparative weakness of his Hasidic beliefs. Louis Jacobs states that while it is difficult to find a set of Hasidic doctrines that are acceptable to all Hasidic sects, there are "certain basic themes and a certain mood, founded on the pantheistic beliefs that are fairly constant. Among the ideas stressed in every variety of Hasidic thought are: the love and fear of God; *devekut*, 'cleaving' to God at all times; *simhah*, 'joy' in God's presence; *hitlahavut*, 'burning enthusiasm' in God's worship; and *shiflut*, 'lowliness,' 'humility,' construed as a complete lack of awareness of the self."[10] It is noteworthy that Danny does not illustrate in his life any of these beliefs or actions. Indeed, his concerns are almost entirely with how he can achieve self-fulfillment and pursue the secular studies for which he has a growing passion. One critic has stated that "Danny", for want of a better word—the word has been overly used and abused, though it applies here—has been alienated—from his father, from Hasidism, and finally from the Hasidic community itself."[11]

Historical events thrust themselves with great force upon the characters. I have already discussed the reactions of Reb Saunders and David Malter to the Holocaust and the rebirth of Israel, events that Potok uses to show basic theological differences between the two men and the two religious groups. Potok also mentions the death of President Roosevelt and devotes most space to the Malters' reaction, with Reuven weeping and his father deeply grieved. They are placed within the context of the typical American reaction to the tragic event, as seen by descriptions of people stunned or crying in the street. Danny feels that the death is a "terrible thing," but we are not given Reb Saunders's reaction. This lack of information heightens the reader's sense of the Hasidic leader's apartness from secular, non-Jewish events. It may show some of Potok's bias in favor of David Malter, who has earlier told Reuven that he "should not forget there is a world outside" (55).

The "world outside" includes those American myths that surround the Jewish communities in the novel, in particular that of the American Dream. Although the Hasidic community tries to insulate itself from American influences, this proves impossible. Danny Saunders's interest in secular subjects and his eventual decision to become a psychologist implies something about the openness of American society to new possibilities; however, the fact that Danny must relinquish his Hasidic identity in order to take advantage of these possibilities also tells us something of the demands that America makes on those who would achieve their dreams there. Sheldon Grebstein observes that despite its strong Jewish content, *The Chosen* is a highly American novel:

Accordingly, the American cultural myth or fable at the heart of *The Chosen* is essentially that of both the Horatio Alger stories and *The Great Gatsby*— the dream of success. In this version the story is played out by an improbable but possible "only in America" cast of Hasidic and orthodox Jews, who demonstrate that people can still make good through hard work, and that severe difficulties can be overcome by pluck, integrity, and dedication. At the story's end the novel's two young heroes are about to realize the reward they have earned: a limitless future. In sum, *The Chosen* can be interpreted from this standpoint as an assertion of peculiarly American optimism and social idealism. Very simply, it says Yes. [12]

Indeed, *The Chosen* does say "Yes" for the two adolescent Jewish boys. Reuven is elected president of his class, receives virtually all A grades, and graduates summa cum laude. He also has the choice of becoming either a mathematician or a rabbi. Danny also graduates summa cum laude; is accepted to do graduate work at Harvard, Berkeley, and Columbia; will become a psychologist; and finds that his father accepts his decision not to inherit the *tzaddikate* but pass it on to his sickly brother instead. This optimism underlies the novel, even at those points where negative elements enter into it. One always has an ultimate belief that the two boys are so basically decent, and are perceived by the author as being so worthy, that in the end their actions will lead to success, and problems which seem very thorny indeed, like Danny's inevitable confrontation with his father over the leadership of the community, will be resolved.

Potok manages to permit the boys to remain strongly Jewish while taking advantage of the opportunities offered by American society. In this he differs from most other Jewish-American authors whose Jewish characters frequently must sacrifice important aspects of their Jewishness in order to take advantage of American opportunity. Indeed, the majority of the characters in twentieth-century Jewish-American writing do not view the relinquishment of their Jewishness as a major sacrifice. Describing a symposium held by the *Contemporary Jewish Record* (*Commentary's* predecessor) in 1944 entitled "American Literature and the Younger Generation of American Jews," David Daiches observes that "Many of the contributors to the symposium seemed to think that their Americanism had subsumed their Judaism. One writer went so far as to equate the 'Declaration of Independence' with certain Jewish prayers, and Lincoln with Hillel."[13]

The enormous effect of the American Dream or, in Danny's case in particular, American opportunity as an inherent aspect of the Dream, is stated in part by Loren Baritz when he writes that the Jew had almost always "managed to resist the particular physical locale of his Galut by remembering his participation both in history and in the Jewish community. But because when we moved to America we responded to a psychological reversal promised by the American Dream—a promise of the end of Galut—we became more susceptible to the incursions of American utopianism, of America's rejection of the past, of age, and of continuity with Europe."[14] While Danny does not take his attraction to American opportunity so far as to reject the past, to reject Judaism, one can see in his rejection of his father's Hasidism an awareness that American society will permit both a secular profession and a Jewish life. However, even America makes demands of those who wish to use its gifts: Danny Saunders cannot retain his Hasidic way of life and his Hasidic appearance and still become a successful psychologist in America. As Baritz also writes: "Because of America's rejection of the past, of the fierce commitment to the notion that this land will start anew, the American Jew is pulled apart. To be a Jew is to remember. An American must forget."[15] Danny must "forget" some of his Hasidic ways.

Reuven Malter has less intense choices to make than Danny since his type of Judaism does not prevent him from entering the secular world while retaining his Jewish identification. Ironically, he decides to become a rabbi and remain totally in a Jewish environment. Reuven, however, is aware of the necessity that some Jews feel to prove their Americanism. As narrator he points out that some of the teachers of non-Jewish subjects ("English teachers") in the Jewish parochial schools felt it necessary to organize competitive baseball leagues "to show the gentile world that yeshiva students were as physically fit, despite their long hours of study, as any other American student" (13). This feeling arises as a result of America's entry into World War II and the desire on the part of most Jews that they should be seen as able to do their part in the war effort. Indeed, because baseball is the quintessential American game, "to the students of most of the parochial schools, an inter-league baseball victory had come to take on only a shade less significance than a top grade in Talmud, for it was an unquestioned mark of one's Americanism, and to be counted a loyal American had become increasingly important to us during these last years of the war" (14). Thus optimism about America does not totally remove the Jews' awareness of their differences from the majority culture or the need to temper the more extreme external manifestations of their faith on the part of those who wish to become more a part of mainstream American society.

Potok has reservations concerning the importance of the American Dream and American optimism in *The Chosen*. He asserts that "A covering hypothesis regarding the popularity of my work should take into account the many Jewish and non-Jewish readers of Potok . . . in France, Germany, England, Holland, Japan, Australia, the Philippines, and elsewhere, including the Soviet Union. What do all those people know about Horatio Alger, . . . American optimism and social idealism, and the American reverence for the pioneer?"[16] This comment appears in an essay in which Potok addresses himself to remarks made by Sheldon Grebstein a year earlier (see note 12). While one can sympathize with Potok's point to a degree, it remains true that with its American setting, the nature of Danny Saunders's belief in what is possible, Reuven Malter's basic faith that his future lies in his own hands, and the ultimate success of these characters and, indeed, of David Malter in achieving his goals, the novel exudes a type of optimism that is strongly associated with

America. That this optimism and level of success can exist elsewhere is not in doubt; that it underlies, indeed pervades, *The Chosen* is what gives the book its American ethos. Non-Americans can appreciate and understand this ethos because of general cultural dissemination of American ideals and, not inconsiderably, because of the attitudes that Potok describes in the novel.

The Value of Education

The Chosen could be viewed as a paean to education. All the central characters are intensely and joyfully engaged in learning, and Potok imbues the quest for knowledge with great excitement. Jews have long placed great value upon learning, with communities in Europe supporting, if at a meager level, Talmud students so that they could pursue their studies. It was felt that a valuable and holy gift for a wealthy man to present to a son-in-law was an extended period of financial support after the marriage so that the young man could engage in study. Supporting a religious scholar was a *mitzvah* (good deed), as his study of the holy books reflected upon the religiosity of the family.

The positive attitude toward education can be seen in the verve with which the protagonists engage in complex discussions of difficult texts. Reuven describes a discussion between Reb Saunders, Danny, and himself thus: "It was a pitched battle. With no congregants around, and with me an accepted member of the family, Danny and his father fought through their points with loud voices and wild gestures of their hands almost to where I thought they might come to blows" (164). They do not come to blows, however, as Reuven realizes that "Reb Saunders was far happier when he lost to Danny than when he won. His face glowed with fierce pride. . . . The battle went on for a long time, and I slowly became aware of the fact that both Danny and his father, during a point they might be making or listening to, would cast inquisitive glances at me, as if to ask what I was doing just sitting there while all this excitement was going on: Why in the world wasn't I joining in the battle?" (165). Reuven does join in and finds that he is "enjoying it all immensely. . . ."

One rarely comes across an author who can convincingly present learning as the most exciting aspect of the lives of adolescents. One does wonder at times whether Potok does not overdo this total commitment to books. Where, for instance, is the boys' awareness of sports, popular music, girls. Have they no hobbies? Neither Reuven nor Danny is particularly interested in baseball despite the opening of the novel, and after Danny tells Reuven that his sister had been "promised" at the age of two to the son of one of his father's followers any interest in girls disappears from the story. Reuven attends her wedding, finds her beautiful, but his concern in this novel for female companionship is over. As one might expect, in the film version of the novel a good deal more is made of Reuven's feelings for Danny's sister. She even seems somewhat attracted to him. As in the novel, however, nothing comes of this attraction.

Although Reuven is not Hasidic, Potok seems to have burdened him with many "Hasidic" restrictions: " 'Youth' does not have high status in the Hasidic community, since it is regarded as only a preliminary to adulthood. . . . Boys and girls do not meet ambiguities and uncertainties concerning their expected behavior, since the role of youth is to obey their elders and behave in a way that is appropriate for Hasidic people."[17] Reuven is certainly freer than Danny in his opportunities to interreact with the secular world and in the fact that he does not feel "trapped" as does Danny. However, because Potok makes Danny a genius and Reuven a near-genius neither boy can be viewed as a representative adolescent.

Both fathers are committed to intellectual pursuits, and the home life of both boys at times resembles a classroom. Indeed, Potok uses the different methods of teaching employed by the fathers to illustrate different approaches to Judaism that are of great importance in the novel. He writes of "the lecture on Hasidism by David Malter to his fifteen year old son (the scientific Western-oriented method of teaching) and the synagogue-set exhortations of Reb Saunders (the traditional Eastern-European method of teaching)."[18] Reb Saunders also engages in Talmudic discussions with his son which, as we have seen, permit disagreement over possible interpretations. These discussions, however, are carried on in private, but, even privately, Reb Saunders would never permit David Malter's method of textual emendation to be used in his presence. In an interview in which Potok was asked what kind of teacher should "teach truths," he replied: "I would say that the teacher should be somebody like Reuven Malter's father. In many ways he exemplifies the Jewish adventure."[19] Education is an inherent part of that adventure in Potok's work.

David Malter is Potok's ideal teacher because despite his Orthodoxy he does not eschew the twentieth century and what it can offer
to his understanding of Judaism. This attitude extends to his method
of teaching his son and to his expectations of the breadth of his
son's interests. Reuven can discuss any topic with his father, although all those discussed are important and worthy ones. David
Malter has a respect for secular knowledge that is lacking in Reb
Saunders, and a regard for analysis of all issues. Reb Saunders's
narrowness, on the other hand, reflects Hasidic views: "If one is
educated in Jewish matters, he will rank high only if his education
is used to intensify his Hasidic behavior. Education in itself, without
Hasidic observances, has little status value. Occupation, income,
and residence, too, carry status value only if they supplement Hasidic
behavior."[20]

The result of these differing attitudes toward education is that
Danny's attempt to pursue secular studies becomes a source for
conflict in the novel whereas Reuven's father is proud of his son's
ability in mathematics. Indeed, although David Malter is proud
that Reuven has decided to become a rabbi, he tells him that he
would have been very pleased if he had decided to become a university professor of mathematics. He knows that Reuven will not
give up his Judaism, and he considers a profession in the secular
world to be honorable and worthwhile.

Reb Saunders's way of educating his son has apparently failed to
give him the "heart" necessary to find the role of *tzaddik* attractive
despite his desire to study psychology and his seeming interest in
the more "human" Freudian approach as opposed to the clinical
orientation of Dr. Applemen, his psychology professor. One critic
observes:

The Saunderses seem to have an excess of head in their (paradoxical streak
of zealousness and emotional) makeup; but the Malters have heart *and*
head: they are in balance. . . .
Reuven's studies are "brain" disciplines—logic, mathematics, philosophy—yet it is he who finally turns out to have more "heart" than the
brilliant son of a Hasid. Danny, on the other hand, having been raised
in the tradition of the Ba'al Shem, should have been a "heart-and-joy
specialist." Yet it is he who is all brain. And this produces a keen irony,
since Hassidism, a movement that was originally a revolt against arid
scholasticism became (as portrayed in *The Chosen*) transformed into its

opposite. Piety, joy, even learning, (a late-comer to Hassidism) becomes pietism, rote learning, memorization.[21]

The results of their educations may have produced quite different people, but Reuven and Danny do share an important set of ideals. Like their fathers they are committed to learning and to its best attributes: thoughtfulness, a desire for self-improvement, and a respect for those whose knowledge is greater than their own. In addition, the sort of learning upon which they devote most of their time is religious in nature. This has given both of them a belief in the importance of morality and of the spiritual aspect of man. In short, their belief in the importance of learning has made both of them decent, caring people who are oriented toward higher things.

It is interesting to note that *The Chosen* appears to appeal to adolescent boys and girls when, as has been pointed out, it is not concerned with what might be thought to be the "normal" interests of this age group. An English teacher in a high school in Midland, Texas (not noted for its high Jewish population), has written that "Although there are some difficult aspects in studying this book in high school, after some preliminary research into the practices of the Jewish religion the students on the junior level read the book and rated it highest in interest of all the major works that we studied this year."[22] The other books studied included *The Red Badge of Courage, Huckleberry Finn,* and *The Old Man and the Sea.*

One can speculate that the appeal of the novel lies in its tapping of the honorable and more "spiritual" side of the adolescent personality. Both Reuven and Danny exhibit a wide range of very admirable traits, and the issues they confront are clearly of importance and have a moral dimension. Also, there is the appeal of the exotic, the sense that information about a secret world is being imparted. Indeed, education of non-Jews and of Jews who are not Hasids provides one of the important appeals of the novel. There are long historical passages, virtually lectures, which David Malter delivers to his son concerning the history of Hasidism and of the Jews. There are exciting Talmudic discussions that culminate in six pages describing a class recitation in which Reuven tackles a very difficult passage in the Talmud using different critical methods. Potok manages to make this recitation gripping in its presentation (it continues over four days of class time) on account of both the subject matter and the understanding that the teacher, Rav Gershenson, is believed not to like the method of textual emendation that Reuven's father uses in his articles and which, finally, Reuven is forced to use himself. Since this teacher will be instrumental in deciding whether or not Reuven is permitted to enter the rabbinate, there is an added tension.

Danny lectures Reuven on the intricacies of Freudian psychology and finds that it is necessary to learn German in order to read Freud in the original. While it might be very difficult for even bright high school pupils to identify with either boy on an academic level because of his brilliance, it is not unreasonable to think that admiration of them would be a common feeling. In regard to Danny's reading of Freud, Potok does create difficulties for him in that even with a knowledge of German he cannot grasp the nuances of the case descriptions. A neat relationship between the Talmud and Freud seems to point the way forward: "He had been going at it all wrong, he said, his eyes bright with excitement. He had wanted to *read* Freud. That had been his mistake. Freud had to be *studied,* not read. He had to be studied like a page of Talmud. And he had to be studied with a commentary" (181).

One critic states that even using this method it is unlikely that Danny could fully understand Freud since "such a boy at his age could not confront the works of Freud in any meaningful way. The problem is not one of intelligence—he might grasp the dictionary meaning of the words—but lack of life experience. . . ."[23] The pupils in Midland, Texas might well have more experience of "life" than does Danny with his cloistered upbringing.

The Chosen is an "education" novel, a bildungsroman. The teenage characters develop in mind and character as time passes, their experiences heightening their understanding of themselves and of their place in the world. This form is a very common one in Jewish-American literature:

> The education novel exactly reproduces the central experience of American Jewry: the movement from the enclosed *shtetl* (Eastern European village) environment, with its highly ordered and pervasive moral system (diffused by peasant lore and a necessarily realistic view of humanity), to the exacting demands of an industrial society. . . . America, coming with such suddenness to so many, intensified the cleavage between the domestic religious culture of the Jews and their external lives in a country which regarded them as an anomaly. The novel repeats the pattern of this

process by describing a youth outgrowing the protection of the home and encountering the beckoning life without.[24]

The world of the Hasids described in *The Chosen* is very similar to that of "the enclosed shtetl" in its imposition upon its members of a rigid moral and behavior code that attempts to ignore that of the majority culture. As we have seen, both Danny and Reuven are greatly influenced by American society, this causing in Danny's case the cleavage of which Sherman writes. The Jewish writer's version of the education or "initiation" novel tends to place more stress upon family relations than does that produced by his non-Jewish counterpart. This, also, can be clearly seen in *The Chosen* as the relations between the Saunderses and the Malters, and between the respective fathers and sons, occupy the center stage.

Fathers and Sons

Book 1 of *The Chosen* begins with the following quotation from "Proverbs": "I was a son to my father . . . / And he taught me and said to me, / 'Let your heart hold fast my words . . .' " (9). This epigraph sets the tone not only for the first section of the novel but for the novel as a whole in that father-son relationships are central to the development of the plot and to an understanding of the various conflicts that occur. The virtual absence of women heightens the centrality of the male relations but, of course, it eliminates any consideration of the complexities of family life, a theme that is very common and important in Jewish-American writing. This somewhat artificial situation (unlike Reuven, Danny has a mother and a sister, but they are almost invisible) parallels the somewhat artificial adolescences of the two boys. A feminine element in the plot would have provided a more balanced family life to offset the male-dominated, religious and educational intensity of the novel.

The stress upon fathers parallels a similar stress in Judaism, where God is King, Judge, and Father. When "authority is involved, God the King or Judge; when He offers love and mercy, even to the wicked, He is Father. Symbolic Hebrew religion deceives some into thinking Deity is really fatherhood."[25] Thus, the father can be viewed as a fount of wisdom, one who takes upon himself some of the aura of the Godhead. This can be clearly seen in Danny's reaction to Reb Saunders and, in terms of respecting his knowledge, ethics, and religiosity, in Reuven's reaction to his father.

One of the sayings of the Baal Shem Tov illustrates the close links between learning, the Godhead, and fatherhood which exists both in Hasidic and non-Hasidic Judaism: " 'The Lord does not object even if one misunderstands what a man learns, provided he only strives to understand out of love of learning. It is like a father whose beloved child petitions him in stumbling words, yet he takes delight in hearing him.' There is honor between father and son. The father is the benevolent teacher; the son is the obedient student."[26] As Malin observes here, the father-son relationship is one of honor and respect, in the words of the Baal Shem Tov. Despite any differences that occur between the fathers and sons in *The Chosen,* a high level of respect remains in force between the father-teacher and his son.

The strength of the two father-son relationships provides a central focus of the novel in that even when rebellion against the father takes place, as it does in Danny's case, the father is not presented in a totally negative light. Potok shows that Reb Saunders's reasons for acting the way he does are not selfish ones but are in the service of higher things: he is seen as a *tzaddik* who suffers for his flock and for the Jewish people and not merely as a tyrannical father. Danny may resent the pressures put upon him by his father, but he still respects and loves him; Reuven has no reason not to love and respect his father, as he is presented as the most admirable character in the novel.

The ways in which the two boys are raised can be seen as reflecting the fanaticism or tolerance of their fathers. Reb Saunders's raises Danny in silence in order to try to give him a suffering soul that will enable him to feel the pain of his people. Danny's brilliant mind is not sufficient in itself for a *tzaddik,* and his father is appalled that as a child Danny seems to lack the human compassion to match his intellectual brilliance. While Reb Saunders is undoubtedly a fanatic, he does suffer greatly because of this method of raising his son. As we have seen he is willing to make the sacrifice in order that a higher cause be served: that of creating the right sort of leader for his people. *A Time for Silence* was the tentative manuscript title of the novel. This shows the importance Potok placed upon silence and its implications for all of the characters, although it has its greatest effect upon Danny and his father.

Reb Saunders's method largely fails in that its primary effect is to drive Danny out of the community and into the secular world. We must wait for *The Promise* to see the positive effects of this method. While a fascination with secular literature explains much of Danny's lack of interest in Hasidism, it seems probable that the harshness of his father's method of raising him contributes to his distaste for both Hasidism and the role of *tzaddik*. One critic feels that Reb Saunders manages virtually to nullify Danny's personality in that "Danny becomes an object, manipulated by his father, rather than a person one relates to."[27] Danny's personality is somewhat flat rather than round, his conflict with his father and Hasidism being more interesting than he is. His ultimate choice of Freudian as opposed to clinical psychology is presented more in scientific than in humanistic terms, in spite of his comments concerning the more "human" appeal to him of the Freudian approach. In his rebellion, Danny reacts to the intolerance of his father.

By contrast, Reuven Malter is raised in an atmosphere of tolerance and love that is exhibited daily rather than assumed to exist without outward signs. However, David Malter is not a *tzaddik* and does not have the responsibilities toward a group of people and the preservation of a dynasty which Reb Saunders does. Because he is not a Hasid, David Malter is not enclosed in a world which makes the sort of extreme demands that Reb Saunders must face daily. Nonetheless, Malter is committed to the preservation of the Jewish people and fights tirelessly for the creation of a Jewish state. His illness and recovery reflect the condition of the Jews as they move from Auschwitz to Israel. He is also an observer of the commandments, which requires a great deal of discipline in his life. His outgoing love for his son and his respect and tolerance for his needs must be seen in relation to his attitude toward Judaism and toward the secular world, attitudes which we have seen to be far different from those of Reb Saunders.

David Malter teaches his son respect for tolerance. He tells him that "Honest differences of opinion should never be permitted to destroy a friendship . . ." (219). He illustrates this attitude in his reaction to Reb Saunders, who has bitterly attacked him because of his stance concerning the creation of the State of Israel. Reb Saunders is a fanatic, he feels, in his anti-Zionist stance and the extent to which he is willing to heap scorn upon those who disagree with him. Yet, when Reuven finds that his hatred of Danny's father is

growing daily, David Malter defends Reb Saunders on account of
his faith and the way in which faith such as his has preserved the
Jewish people through two thousand years of persecution. He prefers
a rational approach: "He disagreed with Reb Saunders, yes, but he
would countenance no slander against his name or his position. Ideas
should be fought with ideas, my father said, not with blind passion.
If Reb Saunders was fighting him with passion, that did not mean
that my father had to fight Reb Saunders with passion" (234). The
difference between the two fathers cannot be more clearly seen than
in this disparate approach toward the treatment of those with whom
one disagrees.

One critic views the two approaches in terms of rationality and
mysticism: "In the crisis of generations and cultures, the son of the
rationalist, who has come to love the tradition because he has been
reared in love, chooses to sustain it; the son of the mystic, reared
in silence and seeming hatred, turns toward secular science."[28] While
the observation is basically sound, one must question whether Reb
Saunders is a mystic, since he places so much stress upon intellectual
analysis of the Talmud and does not exhibit a particularly Kabbalistic
(Jewish mystical) leaning toward religious texts or experience. As
noted earlier, Israel Baal Shem Tov, the founder of Hasidism, was
much concerned with nonintellectual, mystical experiences as a means
of understanding God. Reb Saunders, as indeed Hasidism in general,
has deviated from this total stress upon "simple," mystical experience and has established practices that the Baal Shem would not
have wholeheartedly supported. While most Hasidic groups still
place some emphasis upon religious ecstasy achieved through dance
and certain repetitive tunes (the Hasidic *nign*), particularly for the
mass of Hasidim, they would not differ very much in their regard
for the types of intellectual analysis of Talmudic texts for the more
able among them, as illustrated in the religious discussions between
Danny and his father.

In their concern to pass on the Jewish heritage to their sons, both
fathers use what could be described as "rational" methods. At the
end of the day it is not so much the method used (silence is used
by Reb Saunders as a "rational" method to produce a particular
result) as the underlying feeling of love each boy either sees or does
not in his father which produces the results of which Hochman
writes. The son's awareness of his father's love becomes related to
the son's feeling for the type of Judaism for which the father stands.

To Reuven, Judaism is as much what his father is as it is a tradition and a body of laws and commandments. In choosing to become a rabbi, Reuven reflects both his love of Judaism and the love which his father, as the primary symbol of Judaism in his life, gave to him; in rejecting the *tzaddikate,* Danny reflects both his distaste of the narrow Hasidic world and the lack of love that his father, as the primary symbol of Hasidism in his life, forced him to endure.

Form and Content

Potok's style in *The Chosen* has been criticized for the flatness of the dialogue, the subservience of characterization to thematic considerations, and a degree of contrivance to create a symmetrical plot structure in which various plot developments end in a neat balance. Sheldon Grebstein writes: "Its style ranges from undistinguished to banal. Its tone is subdued and utterly humorless. Its pace is moderate. Its overall color is gray. With all these handicaps that *The Chosen*—this really Jewish book—should have attained best-sellerdom seems more than a phenomenon; it is truly a miracle. But miracle or not, its 38 weeks on the list is an obdurate fact demanding explanation."[29] Before exploring the possible explanations for the novel's popularity, some analysis of these adverse criticisms is necessary.

The dialogue in the novel is uninspiring and very slow-paced; however, the subjects being discussed are often highly intellectual in content. They are historical, religious, moral, or related to the intricacies of personality as exhibited by high-minded and complex individuals. In short, the dialogue is suitable for the subjects and themes that are central to the novel. Where it does fall short is in its lack of differentiation between different characters, there being little subtlety of nuance in the speech patterns of one character as compared to another. Because the tone of the conversations is almost always highly serious, there is a marked lack of the lighter side of the characters' personalities.

This one-sidedness can also be seen in character descriptions. There is a mechanical quality about most of them. To show suppressed emotion, certain characters' eyes frequently become "misty"; others gesticulate wildly when they talk, or "nod vaguely" to show their preoccupation with other matters than the ones being discussed. Moreover, these physical traits are repeated throughout the novel to the point of becoming too predictable.

As Potok himself points out in an article I will discuss shortly, the characters speak Yiddish almost all of the time. Yet, there is no attempt in the novel at mimesis through setting apart the non-English phraseology by syntactical methods or through presenting it in, say, perfect English as does Henry Roth in *Call It Sleep,* another novel in which many of the characters (the Shearl family and most of their neighbors) speak Yiddish almost all of the time.

One aspect of *The Chosen* which could have created difficulties through interference with the narrative line is the educative aspect. There are a number of "lecturettes" concerning Hasidic and Jewish history which, like the cetology chapters of *Moby-Dick,* intrude into the plot. Indeed, one critic has referred to the novel as "documentary fictionalized." She goes on to write that "Claustrophobic reading, and really, description of 'customs and traditions' however well done, are not basically what a novel should concern itself with."[30] Perhaps, but the depiction of "customs and traditions" is both relevant and suitable for *The Chosen.* Indeed, the intrusions into the novel of this material can be regarded as essential to an appreciation of the plot. Not only is reference made to it during other portions of the text, but Potok uses this educative material in part to explain the various actions and beliefs of the characters. It therefore takes on more importance than mere extraneous material would normally have. While it is not dramatized, neither is it just "dead" exposition.

By no means have all critics found *The Chosen* wanting in all respects; many have had positive reactions and at least one discovered that having liked the novel "somewhat" in April, liked it "quite a lot" in June. He goes on to say that *"The Chosen* has stayed in memory and, staying, has grown."[31] Most reviewers have praised the sincerity, warmth, and humanity of the novel and have responded to the decency and believability of characters presented in such a sympathetic manner. As Granville Hicks observes: "it is hard to make good boys interesting; it must have been even harder for Chaim Potok to bring to life a pair of good fathers, good in different ways. But he succeeded, and the result is a fine, moving, gratifying book."[32] Indeed, one of the strongest aspects of the novel is the characters, despite the weakness of the dialogue. They remain interesting as people because of what they represent and the skillful manner in which Potok shows their struggles to reach admirable but difficult goals while remaining ethical individuals. There was a danger that these characters would become allegorical, mere symbols or types, thus losing their individuality and humanness. Potok has avoided this pitfall through the creation of a story so interesting in the moral issues raised, in the conflicts presented, and in the exoticism of its setting and themes that we are caught up in the flow from the narrative which, in turn, lends the characters weight and depth.

Daphne Merkin states that Potok has consciously eschewed the "attempt to write about situations or characters that might stand in for humanity in general, and has concentrated instead on the particular, writing from an insularly Jewish perspective that denies broader implications."[33] Unquestionably, Potok's world in *The Chosen* is firmly rooted in a particular place and culture, the characters illustrating the beliefs and practices of a distinct minority. One can think of many novels about which the same observations could be made. This does not mean that "broader implications" are denied. Isaac Bashevis Singer speaks of the importance of literature having an "address": "I would say that literature must have an address, that it just cannot be in a vacuum. This is very important. Many modern writers would like to get rid of this and write about humanity—general humanity, just abstract human beings. This cannot be done. . . . In other words, literature cannot operate in a void above humanity. It is strongly connected with a group, with a clan. . . ."[34]

If within their particular situations the emotions and reactions of the characters are "true to life," they can be said to exhibit realistic human traits, and Potok is certainly writing within a realistic convention. Indeed, as Sheldon Grebstein points out, "Perhaps its greatest achievement stylistically is its versimilitude, the solidly detailed portrayal of place, time, weather, scene, object, gesture."[35]

The novel is related through the first-person point of view of Reuven Malter, a reliable narrator who, despite his central position in the tale, does not exude infallibility but takes the audience with him in his difficulties in coping with a Hasidic world that is as strange to him as it is to the reader. Reuven mirrors the reader's emotions as he tries to figure out how to cope with Reb Saunders and remain the ethical person whom his father has tried to create. Reuven and David Malter illustrate the plight of any tolerant individual come face to face with intolerance, the doubts and hesitations of the narrator and the advice of his father providing paradigms of a struggle for decency which has universal implications. Reb Saunders illustrates the plight of a man intimately concerned with ethics whose goals, honorable though they may be, cause him to feel justified in using highly dubious means in their attainment. Not an evil man, he exemplifies the complexities involved in moral decisions. His ghettolike world and sense of absolute sureness render him almost impervious to the force of contrary argument. This is his tragedy and that of his son who must attempt self-fulfillment within the narrow world of absolutes that his father hands down or who must leave that world for another.

In an essay entitled "A Reply to a Semi-Sympathetic Critic," Potok attempted to answer the criticisms of his work stated by a number of critics but, in particular, those of Sheldon Grebstein. He states that in a novel he prefers "simplicity to complexity" and compares his problem with dialogue to that faced by Ernest Hemingway. Just as he had to decide how to present the Yiddish which his characters speak almost all of the time, Hemingway had to decide how to communicate in English the Italian and Spanish of, respectively, *A Farewell to Arms* and *For Whom the Bell Tolls,* as well as these languages in various short stories. Potok writes that "He solved it in his way (and it has been said of him too that all his characters sound alike), and I solved it in mine. Style is the right word in the right place, as Jonathan Swift pointed out."[36]

While Potok's dialogue is not as evocative as Hemingway's spare, stripped syntax, Hemingway's influence is clear and frequently results in our being aware of wider implications in the understated phraseology that fills *The Chosen.* Unfortunately, this awareness often fails to occur. When Potok has a character say nothing in response to a statement about which we know he has strong feelings, the effect can be that we fill in the gaps, as Potok probably intends, or that we feel something important has been omitted, the author having taken the easy way out. The problem arises when we do not feel that there is enough information for the gaps to be filled or that the technique is too transparent. Indeed, this problem occurs, at times, in Hemingway's writing as well; however, he manages to make the style work far more frequently than does Potok in this novel.

Potok points out how painstakingly his novels are written, with numerous revisions and rewritings. He says that he uses "a kind of talked style . . . and one would do well to remember who the 'talkers' are in each of the novels and the extent to which their style of talking varies within the limitations of simplicity I have set for them."[37] He is correct when he says that one must remember who the "talkers" are. One tends to change the word stresses in one's own mind according to how one understands the personality of the character who is speaking. While he does provide verbal clues to some speech patterns (Reb Saunders and Rav Gershenson, in *The Promise* both use "Nu," meaning "Well?" or "What?" when they speak), Potok does not make syntactical changes to imitate Yiddish speech patterns as does Bernard Malamud or, as I have mentioned, use flawless English as does Henry Roth. It may well be that reliance upon characterization, without appropriate changes in the diction and syntax of the various speakers, in order to distinguish speech differences is inadequate—too much reliance being placed upon the subjectivity of the reader. Although Potok's style does work to an extent, "simplicity" can be taken too far.

The popularity of *The Chosen* is due to a number of factors, not least of which is the exoticism of its setting. Both Jews and non-Jews found the descriptions of the Hasidic world in particular to be fascinating. This closed world had not been presented before in such an accessible manner or with such interesting characters as Reb Saunders and Danny. The educative aspect of the novel aided its popularity in that readers were not only being told a story with an interesting plot but were learning something at the same time. I have already discussed the optimism and American social idealism that fills the book and supports the American predelection for believing that hard work and decency are rewarded in the end. One must not forget, either, the quality of the presentation of the conflicts in the novel or the appeal of the moral tone with which these conflicts are presented. *The Chosen* achieved best-sellerdom through a stress upon morality, learning, and sincerity presented by unusual characters who inhabit a strange world and in whom the author obviously believes. Far from being a shortcoming, the lack of violence, sexuality, and deceit in the novel proved to be a strong recommendation.

It is interesting to note what changes to the novel the filmmakers thought necessary in order to widen its appeal even further. In addition to the increased romantic interest between Reuven and Danny's sister referred to earlier, the Hasidim are made less objectionable. The notion of Danny's trying to kill Reuven in a baseball game that the Hasidim have turned into a Holy War is absent from the film. Religiosity is toned down. Although Reuven attends a seminary and says that he wants to become a rabbi, we never see either he or his father praying. Reuven occasionally wears a skullcap; his father never does. The stress is upon the contrast between the Americanized Malters and utterly un-Americanized Saunders and Hasidim.

Reb Saunders is portrayed somewhat harsh, particularly in relation to Zionism, but his sympathetic aspects are stressed in Rod Steiger's performance. As a result of omission of the information that Danny's brother is permitted to take on the *tzaddikate,* the crisis created by Danny's refusal is not satisfactorily resolved.

The strongest aspect of the film is its atmosphere and verisimilitude. The setting and characters inspire believability (Potok himself appears briefly as a Talmud teacher). It is not as effective as the novel in the creation of the religious conflict but does nonetheless remain remarkably close to the book in its depiction of intra-Jewish and Jewish-American tensions.

Chapter Three
The Promise
The World of Study and Teachers

The Promise is a sequel to *The Chosen* and depicts the results of the choices which were made in the earlier novel. A *Time* magazine reviewer moans that *The Promise* consisted of material which was excised from 800 pages of the original manuscript of *The Chosen,* Potok's editor reviving it for use in this "stultifying" second novel. Potok denies this charge and states that "All of it was written after *The Chosen* was published. . . . The parts of *The Chosen* that my editor and I cut from the original manuscript have not been and never will be published."[1] Reuven and Danny are still students, though now on the graduate level: Danny working for his doctorate in psychology and Reuven for his rabbinical ordination and a master's degree in philosophy. The plot, similar in this respect to that of *The Chosen,* is concerned with tolerance and intolerance, commitment to different interpretations of Jewish law and practice.

Reuven has been taught text criticism of the Talmud by his father; that is, the validity of making textual changes where scholarly evidence shows that the text is in error. This is tantamount to heresy to Rav Kalman, upon whose judgment depends Reuven's ordination. Further to the "left" than the Malters is Abraham Gordon, a scholar who is trying to "regard the tradition critically *and* with love."[2] The Malters and Gordon are bitterly attacked by Rav Kalman, who sees their methods as undermining the traditions for which his students in Europe, and almost himself, died in the concentration camps. Constant reference is made to his rigidity, and while he is also given some sympathetic treatment because of his firm stand for beliefs which he views as essential to Judaism, there is an implicit comparison between his treatment of his "enemies" and that meted out by Senator Joseph McCarthy, whose witch hunts provide a backdrop to the main action.

A major plot strand deals with the mental illness of Abraham Gordon's son Michael. Under supervison by a senior psychologist,

Danny Saunders is treating him and proposes the use of isolation and silence to break down Michael's resistance to telling the therapists his deepest fears and hatreds. This method owes no small debt to Danny's own experiences with silence. The implication is that even so extreme a method used in *The Chosen* by Reb Saunders on Danny for specific quasi-religious reasons can have some secular, even scientific relevance in extreme cases.

Boy-girl relationships constitute a subplot in that Reuven is gently rejected by Rachel Gordon for Danny. Much is made of the coming together of the former Hasid and the daughter of two modern college professors. Rachel is also the niece of the arch-liberal Bible critic Abraham Gordon, and this provides an opportunity for a hint of the possibility of some reconciliation between the opposing religious camps, as Danny is still Orthodox if not Hasidic.

As in *The Chosen* the ending is on an optimistic note, Potok reaffirming the basic decency of the characters despite David Malter's being forced out of his school because of resistance to his ideas on the part of Orthodox newcomers. Even those characters who exhibit fanaticism are seen to be fanatical in the service of deeply held, honorable beliefs, although the damage which they do to individuals is condemned.

In a review of *The Promise,* Lillian Elkin comments: "When the second novel is a sequel, as is *The Promise,* the problem is compounded. The reader searches for beloved characters and may discover that they are now minor ones. His willingness to accept the change is crucial. The author must, in a sense, compete against his previous success."[3] Although Danny's story is important, the novel leans toward Reuven, and his character remains much the same as before; that is, he is intelligent, trustworthy, studious, and highly motivated. There are no surprises in his presentation, and those readers who were curious about his possible development after *The Chosen* should find themselves on familiar ground. When we see him courting Rachel Gordon, he is as well-behaved as we would expect. Even when she leaves him for Danny, he does not permit his emotions full expression; indeed, he even feels some guilt over feeling jealous at all. As in the earlier novel, Reuven is permitted anger and passion concerning religious differences, here with Rav Kalman. His father must again provide a moderating influence, as he did in relation to Reb Saunders, pointing out possible reasons for Rav Kalman acting the way he does. Despite occasional expressions of anger, Reuven verges on being too good to be true.

David Malter plays a smaller role in this novel than in *The Chosen* but is, again, consistently good. Toward the ultra-Orthodox new-comers, who eventually succeed in driving him from the Yeshiva which he helped to found and has taught in for twenty-four years, he shows his displeasure in very mild language. Although fighting back, he keeps his passions firmly in check. His character is consistent in both novels.

He possessed great appeal in the earlier novel on account of his wisdom and tolerance. While he was not a fully rounded character, he did possess sufficient moral qualities to make him the ethical center of the novel and sufficient emotional qualities to render him a believable human being. In relation to *The Promise,* Elkin remarks that "David Malter never achieves a blood and flesh quality. . . . Perhaps, if he had been given a struggle to maintain his under-standing and goodness, he would have emerged far more credible for most of us with human failings."[4] This judgment is not entirely fair in that Elkin seems unwilling to accept her own advice that one should be willing to accept the change in the prominence of characters between *The Chosen* and its sequel. In *The Promise,* David Malter is decidedly a minor character, and while one cannot elim-inate one's knowledge of his more fleshed out characterization in the previous work, one must judge *The Promise* as a novel in its own right which makes different demands upon those characters who are carried forth from the earlier book.

Danny Saunders is now involved much more with psychological than with religious issues, although there are relationships made between the two. He still practices Judaism, but his role in *The Promise* focuses upon his position as a junior therapist intimately involved in Michael Gordon's welfare. In his concern for his patient, he can be seen to have developed the ability to suffer which his father attempted to teach him through raising him in slence in *The Chosen.* Indeed, when Reuven asks him about Reb Saunders' reaction to Rachel's being a Gordon, he says:

"I don't give a damn about her being a Gordon."
"Your father will give a damn."
"I'm not worried about my father. I'm worried about Michael." (134)

Danny's worry about Michael is made very apparent throughout the novel, and his concern is more than just a scientific one: he has developed a suffering soul. Reb Saunders's method has worked, but we see that he and Danny still do not talk to each other. Now they cannot, perhaps because they have never learned how to. Reb Saunders is a sad figure, no sense of his stature and presence appearing in this novel.

Much of *The Promise* revolves around study, religious and secular. As in *The Chosen*, Potok is able to imbue learning with excitement and make it an integral part of the plot and the characters' development. All of the main characters are directly involved in learning of a very high level and are dedicated to ideas that have come out of their studies. Much space is devoted to Abraham Gordon's ideas and various characters' opinions of them. Not only Danny, his father, and Rav Kalman but Reuven and David Malter reject them. The difference lies in the intensity of the rejection and the reactions to Abraham Gordon as an individual. Reuven reads all of Gordon's books and finds them fascinating. His father has also read them and says that "There is more to religion than sociology and anthropology. . . . They are very radical ideas" (63). Reuven tells him that he likes Gordon's questions but not his answers, thus showing a balance of approach.

Reuven is studying in an Orthodox yeshiva, which makes severe demands upon its students' beliefs; particularly demanding is Rav Kalman, his Talmud teacher, who believes that Gordon is a threat to Judaism. We see, however, that both Reuven and his father react strongly against the unknown reader who has written on the title page of one of Gordon's books, "This is the book of an apostate. Those who fear God are forbidden to read it" (63). This reflects the extremism of the ultra-Orthodox, and David Malter's reaction shows where his son has received some of the influences that have shaped his attitudes: "He became angry. 'It should read "those who fear ideas," not "those who fear God." There are times when those who fear God make themselves very unpleasant as human beings' " (63).

Potok presents Abraham Gordon's ideas as a humanistic, anti-supernatural interpretation of Judaism. His questions reflect an attempt to come to grips with modern thought while remaining attached to Jewish culture. If modern scientific discoveries make it impossible to preserve a literal interpretation of the Bible, can one still remain a Jew who accepts Jewish tradition? How far can one bring traditional Jewish beliefs into line with twentieth-century thought and still preserve Judaism's unique vision? Gordon fears that unless some way is found to make religion more directly applicable to the lives of young people, then it may be doomed. In his lectures to university students, he finds a lack of willingness or ability to accept revelation; indeed, he finds that he cannot accept it either, and a faith in a personal God—a God who is concerned with the fate of each human being—is something in which he cannot believe. Yet the tradition is important to him, and he wishes to preserve it. In Abraham Gordon's dilemma can be seen the elucidation of a problem that affects many twentieth-century Jews and which Reform Judaism in the nineteenth century faced as well; that is, can Judaism be interpreted in such a way that Jews will desire to continue an active attachment to it?

Gordon's problem is not one which concerns Rav Kalman, by far the most interesting character in the novel. Like Reb Saunders in *The Chosen,* Rav Kalman is a fanatical believer in his particular type of ultra-Orthodox Judaism and does not hesitate to defend it even if that means that individuals are hurt in the process. He feels that he is preserving Judaism, something that takes precedence over consideration of the needs of individuals. His detestation of Abraham Gordon and his ideas is total, as he believes that Gordon's ideas will destroy Torah Judaism. Potok makes it clear where his feelings lie in that despite Gordon's books being vilified by Rav Kalman and his followers, Gordon understands and can appreciate their zealousness. He tells his wife that many "beautiful ideas" were taught in the Eastern European yeshivas which shared Rav Kalman's viewpoint and that the concentration camps destroyed his faith in man. Gordon is an example of that sympathetic human understanding that Potok often presents as illustrating the true spirit of Judaism, that spirit which, perhaps ironically is often lacking in those characters who adhere to fundamentalist religious beliefs.

Potok has written that "Theology has its origins in the anguish that is felt when one's commitment to a particular religious model of reality is confronted by new knowledge and experiential data that threaten the root assumptions of the model."[5] Both Abraham Gordon and Rav Kalman have this difficulty in *The Promise.* Only Gordon, however, is able to confront it in a creative manner and attempt to form a new model which takes into account the new scientific data. There is the danger, however, that he has gone too far.

Rav Kalman sees Gordon as representative of America where, he says disdainfully, "everything is called Yiddishkeit . . ." (108). His model is the world of East European Judaism that disappeared with the Nazis. Reuven is correct in thinking that Rav Kalman would like to form his yeshiva in America exactly in the mold of the rigid totalitarian one of his youth. Reuven reacts strongly against his fear of secularism and his desire to turn Judaism into a "mental ghetto." The extremes represented by both Abraham Gordon and Rav Kalman cannot provide a sastisfactory approach to the problems faced by Judaism in American secular society. Here as elsewhere Potok rejects the extremes of right or left. Danny refers to Abraham Gordon's method as "freezing," and Reuven to Rav Ralman's ways as "choking." As in *The Chosen* it is the middle path represented by David Malter, and in addition in *The Promise* by Rav Gershenson, that is the best. Potok's own choice of Conservative Judaism, which values tradition but does not avoid consideration of modern thought, is reflected in the preferred approaches of Judaism toward the modern world that are stated or implied in the novels.

Reuven is not alone in feeling the sting of Rav Kalman's criticism, criticism which could result in his not being granted *smicha* (ordination). David Malter also must cope with Rav Kalman's fundamentalist attitudes. While one feels that there is perhaps somewhat too much plot contrivance here, the central conflict in the novel— that of fundamentalism versus qualified traditionalism—is heightened by David Malter's battle against both Rav Kalman's harsh criticisms of his book and the attacks of his followers at his school.

Rav Kalman cannot accept David Malter's critical method because he feels that it would destroy the Torah Judaism in which he has believed all his life and in which his students believed when they were murdered in the concentration camps. Their deaths can only be justified by his defense of a tradition that is fixed and immutable. David Malter, like Abraham Gordon, can empathize with Rav Kalman; indeed, when Reuven's disgust at Rav Kalman's harshness becomes apparent, his father speaks to him of the importance of teachers and the necessity of showing Rav Kalman respect. He points out that Reuven does not know Rav Kalman well enough to call him "detestable." This ability to turn the other cheek characterizes David Malter here as in *The Chosen*. It is a trait that Rav Kalman cannot show because of his past, although Potok does not entirely succeed in tempering our criticism of him on this account; it seems unlikely that he intends to.

The clash of ideas is made very clear in Rav Kalman's reaction to David Malter's book on the Talmud. Reuven calls it "vicious," and as first-person narrator cites the main criticisms if Rav Kalman's review:

> If one accepted the possibility of changing .the text of the Talmud, then what might happen to the laws that were based on these texts?. . . . Why not change the text of the Ten Commandments or the various other legal passages? What then would happen to the sanctity of the Bible? How was one to regard the Master of the Universe if one could simply go ahead and rewrite the Bible? How was one to regard the revelation at Sinai? The entire fabric of the tradition would come apart as a result of this kind of method. It was a dangerous method, an insidious method; it could destroy the very heart of Yiddishkeit. . . . Had Jews suffered two thousand years for a tradition based on texts that were filled with scribal errors? (228–29)

This criticism illustrates the basic difference in approach between Rav Kalman and David Malter. Rav Kalman believes that both the Bible and the Talmud, both the Written Law and the Oral Law, are sacred; that there is no distinction in terms of sanctity between them. Using the critical method on one leads naturally, in his estimation, to its use on the other. Rav Kalman and his followers believe that the Oral Law is fixed and cannot be emended. The Malters cannot accept this stance because, as Reuven explains: "There were too many variant readings, too many obvious scribal errors, too many emendations and substitutions of texts even within the Talmud itself for us to believe that text was frozen. We saw the Talmud as containing almost a thousand years of ideas and traditions that had been in flux . . ."(321).

Neither David Malter nor Reuven have any intention of applying the critical method to the Bible, which they accept as having come to the Jews through revelation. In 1974, Potok said: "Reuven Malter will take text criticism up to a certain boundary. He will not cross with it into the biblical period. He will take a text of Talmud and tear it apart and put it together again. But he won't do the same thing with the Hebrew Bible."[6] As we have seen, however, Rav Kalman cannot permit new thought to question the surety of his position as a defender of Torah. He feels that it is acceptable to use Reuven to provide information that he will later use in criticizing his father's book, and Reuven's detestation of Rav Kalman causes him to wonder whether he can receive *smicha* from him without lying—something he is not willing to do. David Malter's reaction is one of helpless rage, " 'They are so rigid,' he said in a sudden angry voice. 'Why do they not see that this rigidity turns away our greatest minds?' " (178).

The critical method that the Malters use is based upon the work of a number of eminent Talmudists, most having done their work in the nineteenth century and later, but some a good deal earlier. Solomon Ben Jehiel Luria worked in the sixteenth century and showed great independence in his teachings and rulings on the Law. He studied commentaries written both before his time and by his contemporaries and based his understanding of religious Law upon these as well as upon those sources of the *Talmud* that he was able to find. He avoided the sort of strained interpretations *(pilpul)* that Reuven tells us Rav Kalman must engage in in order to try to explain Talmudic texts which may well have certain errors in them. He was well respected by other scholars, who accepted his glosses and textual emendations of the Talmud but was viewed with alarm by many teachers in Polish yeshivas who routinely engaged in *pilpul* as, indeed, he himself did in his own yeshiva but only as an exercise to train his students' minds. [7]

The critical method developed more adherents in the nineteenth century with the work of scholars such as Hirsch Mendel Ben Solomon Pineles. He claimed to be a traditionalist whose major concern was to strike a blow against those later commentators who he believed had distorted the *Mishnah* (the legal traditions written down about 200 *C.E.*). His interpretations, often differing from these commentators, brought down upon him the wrath of the traditionalists who felt, as does Rav Kalman, that the explanations given by the later *amoriam* (literally "speakers" whose discussions of the *Mishnah* came to be called the *Gemara*) could not be interfered with by later scholars. He argued, as does Reuven, that he wanted to support the clear meaning of the *Mishnah* against attempts to devalue or misrepresent its meaning. [8]

In the twentieth century, Jacob Nahum Epstein was greatly concerned to establish an accurate version of the *Mishnah* and, as David Malter, used the tools of modern scholarship to clarify obscure passages. He also wanted to establish an accurate text for the Palestinian *Talmud.* [9]

It is the work of these and other scholars which the Malters study in order better to understand the intracacies of the *Talmud.* The problems that they have with traditionalists are similar to those faced by their predecessors who used this method of study. When David Malter's book is due to be published and some of the "fiercely Orthodox" teachers in his school get hold of an advance copy, he is savagely criticized by them, and the staff at his yeshiva split into two opposing camps. His life at his school becomes a nightmare as the newcomers try to prevent him publishing the book. Reuven also faces battles at his own school which, similarly, breaks into factions for and against David Malter's ideas, in favor of Rav Kalman's criticisms or against them. David Malter puts these battles into perspective when he tells Reuven that "Each generation thinks it fights new battles. But the battles are the same. Only the people are different." (235).

The tensions in the novel depend upon those built up through the conflicts between the ideas firmly held by the various teachers who populate the book. Even so mild a character as Rav Gershenson, who is not attacked directly by Rav Kalman and could remain a bystander, is described having a fierce battle with Rav Kalman outside the synagogue of the school. The proximity to the synagogue is no accident, as Rav Gershenson accuses Rav Kalman of wanting to make everyone a saint and of destroying the Torah. He goes on to tell him that "You are destroying people with your religiousity!" (259).

He, like David Malter and Abraham Gordon, expresses the humanistic aspect of Judaism that must be considered in any plea for religious purity. Each of these characters, and eventually Reuven as well, can appreciate what Rav Kalman and his followers suffered in Europe; they can feel compassion for them. Because of this suffering, Rav Kalman and his followers cannot accept their adversaries as sincere Jews deserving of respect. They cannot engage in reasoned argument and debate over matters that must be held sacrosanct because of those who died believing in them.

Speaking of his own experiences as a student, Potok has said:

I'm not sympathetic to Rav Kalman, I'm trying to understand him. When I was in Rav Kalman's class I hated him. When I wrote about him,

I discovered that I would be false to my art if I didn't really try to understand him. And it dawned on me that this was a man full of pain, that every time I had asked him a question the man had cringed inside because he didn't have the answers. This was a man who had lost his family in a concentration camp. He had staked everything on the system of values that had cost him his family's life. What right did I have as an artist to paint him in one dimension as all black and evil? So I dug down into him and tried to understand him.[10]

Potok well understands the implications of this problem. He has written that "A minority culture striving to maintain a viable and creative presence in the midst of a rich majority culture will inevitably find itself in a constant state of war. The battles of that war are fought from lecture podiums, in periodicals and books and classrooms; and across kitchen tables. The weapons are words; casualties can be high; often what is at stake is existence itself—the existence of a proud, identifiable self without which no man is truly human and no people can survive."[11]

Potok does present occasional instances of peace in the midst of this "war." These occur, however, only between the more liberal of the combatants or those who have developed ties of friendship. Thus, David and Reuven Malter can disagree with Abraham Gordon's ideas, yet still see him as a sincere man and be quite willing to discuss ideas with him. Because of friendship, Reb Saunders will not help Rav Kalman in his attack upon David Malter's book, despite his strong abhorrence of scientific criticism. Danny is engrossed in his studies in psychology but still desires Reuven to bring him a copy of the book because he is happy at his former mentor's success in publication. It is doubtful whether he would agree with David Malter's ideas, but friendship can override theological differences in these instances.

When Reuven visits Abraham Gordon's school, he sees a mixture of the traditional and the modern. Gordon and he ritually wash their hands and recite the traditional blessing before their meal, while around them "conversation filled the room. I heard a heated discussion about the relevance of traditional Jewish law to the modern world, another discussion about the way a professor had rearranged a chapter of Hosea earlier that morning, a third discussion about the advantages and disadvantages of small-town pulpits—all of it going on at tables near us. I noticed some people eating without skullcaps and wondered whether they were students or outsiders" (224). A man whom Gordon calls "one of the greatest Talmudists in the world," comes to the table to praise David Malter's book as "a great contribution."

David Malter will, eventually, be driven out of his own school to be welcomed at the Zechariah Frankel Seminary. The freedom of discussion there in which all topics can be examined is much more to his liking than the closed and intolerant world that has come to exist at his own school. He is, however, in the middle: neither a fundamentalist nor a Reconstructionist. He is a liberal Orthodox Jew or, like Potok, a Conservative, one who reflects the ideas of intellectual inquiry combined with largely traditional observance that were espoused by Zechariah Frankel in the nineteenth century. It is not so much differences of belief that determine at which school he can teach as it is differences in the level of tolerance for sincerely held points of view. Potok's primary plea in *The Promise* is not for theological homogeneity but for forbearance and sufferance.

Psychology and the Former Hasid

In *The Chosen,* Danny Saunders made the agonizing choice to give up his inheritance of his father's role and become a psychologist. In *The Promise,* we see him as both student and therapist; however, the past has not been without its effect, and many of the issues revolving around Danny in this novel hark back to the earlier one. Reuven observes that Danny is "obsessed by his hunger to attain perfection in the profession for which he had broken with the *tzaddikate*" (67–68). He allows no room in his life for anything save eating, sleeping, and studying. Even his first patient is seen in terms of the decision he made in *The Chosen:* "Michael was his first attempt at self-vindication, the first in a long series of efforts to prove to himself that the pain he had caused his father at refusing to take on the *tzaddikate,* and the years the *tzaddikate* would ultimately take from his brother's frail life, was all worthwhile" (231). Even Danny's brother Levi asks Reuven if his brother will be "a great psychologist." Levi also wants to know if his own sacrifice will be worthwhile.

Danny is driven to succeed, and his devotion to Michael is comprised of a mixture of his obsession for success and the positive result of Reb Saunders's having raised him in silence. He is presented as having the suffering soul for which Reb Saunders's sacrificed the joys of fatherhood and Danny's childhood. Danny goes to the treatment center on the Sabbath; he prays when Michael is placed in the room alone. He tells Reuven that " 'You don't want to make mistakes with people. Sometimes when you make a mistake you lose a human soul.' He used the Hebrew word *'neshamah'* for the soul . . ." (136). The mixture of the psychologist's caution and the religious man's concern for the sanctity of human life is clear. Indeed, it is this very combination of traits in Danny that causes Abraham Gordon to be willing to permit him to try his experiment on his son.

If we wonder whether it is primarily his drive to succeed or a genuine feeling for humanity that rules his actions, Potok has Rachel Gordon tell Reuven that "Danny had really overwhelmed them a little with his warmth and the patient way he had answered their questions" (89). It does appear that Danny is on the way to becoming something of the "tzaddik for the world" which Reb Saunders's referred to in *The Chosen;* that is, by leaving the narrow world of Hasidism and using his talents in the secular world, Danny's genius—and his heart—have been made available to mankind.

Potok makes clear that Danny's Hasidic background has had an important effect upon him. This is recognized by Abraham Gordon, who feels that Danny is "still very much a Hasid. . . ," though more a Lubavitch Hasid, an "enlightened" Hasid, than a member of his father's more rigid (perhaps Satmar) sect. In deciding whether to grant Danny permission to try his very experimental type of therapy on his son, Gordon tries to evaluate Danny's soul rather than his mind, saying that "when you meet him and discover his sensitivity, his soul, you really begin to understand how remarkable he is. I needed someone I could trust" (226). It is noteworthy that Reb Saunders was also primarily concerned with the state of his son's soul, that aspect of his character having most to do with religion being the basis upon which he is judged by both his fundamentalist father and the modernist Gordon. Despite his intellectual brilliance as a student of psychology, a fact Gordon is aware of, religious and human values are those that are presented as the most important, even in what might be taken to be primarily a scientific intellectual area.

There is some plot contrivance in that, as one critic points out, "One questions whether a graduate student in psychology might be permitted the responsibility of an unorthodox treatment involving a very sick boy even under the supervision of a more experienced psychologist. But the plot is dramatic, often melodramatic, and manages to provide the story that once again links together the destinies of Reuven and Danny."[12] Dr. Altman, Danny's supervisor, thinks that he could do original work in psychology, and Danny points out to Reuven that, as a student, "They would trust his judgement only just so far" (97). However, Elkin's point is well taken. In order to present Danny directly involved in the area for which he gave up so much, Potok has had to stretch a point. Also, as *The Promise* is a sequel to *The Chosen,* the curiosity of readers as to the result of Reb Saunders's method of raising his son in silence had to be satisfied to some extent. By placing Danny in a situation in which intellectual and compassionate qualities were demanded in varying degrees, Potok could show to what extent Danny's character had developed in either direction. Presenting him as having developed a "suffering soul" not only partially vindicates Reb Saunders but provides some justification for a highly dubious method of child rearing, if only in the unique situation in which Danny and his father found themselves.

Michael Gordon is suffering from a mental illness that has its roots in the religious conflicts which pervade the novel. He hates the Orthodox because of their intense criticism of his father and is aware that Rav Kalman is one of his father's harshest critics. Michael goes to a modern yeshiva, but many of the students there are Orthodox, and he considers them "vicious" because of the way in which they express their ideas: "They think they're God over Judaism. They stamp on you like you're a bug if you don't agree with them" (54). Of course, Michael's illness causes him to express attitudes in a much harsher tone than might otherwise be expected; however, as we have seen, the intolerance of the Orthodox fundamentalists affects even so pacific a character as David Malter. The hatred of the Orthodox is, as Reuven says, "The symptom, not the disease." Michael's real problem is more complex and is related to feelings of hatred of his father, this also being related to a Jewish theme.

In his presentation of Danny's highly controversial method of treating Michael, Potok's linking of the religious and scientific provides both plot unity and a connection to the previous novel. Danny is interested in the Kotzker Rebbe, a nineteenth-century Hasidic rabbi near Lublin who spent the last twenty years of his life shut up in his room. He is also reading books and articles concerned with solitude. This reading is to prepare him for Michael's treatment, which will have certain similarities to his own experience at the hands of his father. To remind us of this, there is a discussion in which Reuven explains to Rachel what it means to be raised in silence, how it was done by only a very few Hasidic families and in exceptional circumstances. Potok is presenting this exceptional method of child rearing as a tool which would be of use to a modern psychologist; that is, a traditional religious method can have relevance to a twentieth-century science.

In order to overcome the feeling that this is too farfetched a situation to accept, Potok has provided a number of discussions that revolve around the use of this method of silence as therapy. In discussing Michael with Reuven, Danny says that he "can't get to him with talk. There's a thick shell around him and I can't get through it" (188). Danny will try an experiment on Michael (when Rav Kalman hears of this he is reminded of things that were done to him in the concentration camps; Reuven, also, is appalled); he will try to break him down so that he will talk about his problems and can begin therapy.

As the experiment progresses, there are further allusions to Danny's past: "Danny sat beside me, gazing at Michael, and there was on his face a look of pain and anguish and suffering, as if he were somehow inside Michael, peering out at me through Michael, and I had come to talk to him in his entombing silence" (341). The sympathy Danny feels here is due both to his remembrance of his own sufferings in childhood because of the silence between him and his father and on account of the suffering soul which that experience has given him. A direct relationship is made between Danny, Reuven, and Michael in that each is seen to have had his relationship with his father adversely affected by some aspect of his Jewish experience—Orthodox fanaticism. This provides another unifying element in the novel in that three main characters are related not only in terms of suffering parental conflict but also in thematic terms.

Reuven asks Danny, "Can a son hate a father and not know it?" He is referring to Michael, but Danny's reaction is very personal and dramatic: "He was so startled by the question that I thought he would cry out. He became rigid on the seat and gaped at me. It was a moment or two before I felt him begin to relax" (251).

Danny admits that this is Michael's problem; he also admits, tacitly, that he has had a similar problem. Later, he states openly that "I went through some of that myself a while ago" (351). Danny's hatred of his father could not be acknowledged because of his respect and love for him. These contradictory, unspoken feelings parallel those of Michael Gordon toward his father. He detests him for writing articles and books that draw down upon him the wrath of the Orthodox. This wrath, directed at himself in school as Abraham Gordon's son, makes him detest Judaism because the Orthodox attack him in its name, yet his father loves the religion. Despite this, he loves his father. It is the Orthodox fundamentalists who have twisted his beliefs and love into rage: "How can you love a religion that makes people hate other human beings? I hated it. . . . And my father is trying to teach it" (347). Potok moves the theme of Orthodox intolerance from the purely religious sphere to the personal one.

We are surprised to discover that even Reuven's relationship with his father has been infected by the Orthodox—and particularly Rav Kalman's—invective. Because of Rav Kalman's hostility to David Malter's book, and to the critical method that he has taught to Reuven, Reuven has had great difficulties at school, even his ordination being in doubt. His father asks him:

> "Haven't you hated me during these past months?" he asked softly.
> I hesitated. "It wasn't really—"
> "Why didn't you tell me, Reuven?" (352)

It is on account of Reuven's personal experience with Rav Kalman and his awareness of what it has done to his feelings for his father that he is able to say those things that will bring Michael Gordon out of his shell. We have seen how Danny's experience with silence has sensitized him to suffering and given him an insight into the possible effect of this method on his patient. One critic sums up this bringing together of the psychological and religious spheres: "Reuven and Danny must reconcile themselves to their fathers by acknowledging their hostility to them—precisely what Michael is unable to do. He is, in a sense, their doppelgänger. Their growing comprehension of his sickness enables them to understand themselves. But understanding is not enough. They must act. And each must do so in a way that effectively utilizes what their fathers have imposed on them. That is, they must accept their respective traditions, imbue them with personal vitality and pass them on."[13]

Style

One critic thinks that *The Promise,* unlike *The Chosen,* suffers from a problem of "voice," it being "more studied, balanced, controlled, and consequently less compelling."[14] It has also been said that "Mr. Potok's problem is his sensibility—a fatal deficiency, considering his craft. In Mr. Potok's case, the sensibility which is father to language is Jewish-American genteel, and academic to the bone."[15] Potok, as noted earlier, has admitted to favoring the flattened, studied style that many critics find uncompelling. He feels that its "calculated simplicity" hides implications just beneath the surface. As in *The Chosen,* we are aware of a serious, caring, ultimately unemotional and highly intellectual intelligence ordering the material in *The Promise.* While it is suitable at times, there are numerous instances where it is too heavy and "academic."

As in *The Chosen,* there is also a tendency in *The Promise* to attempt to achieve levels of implication from silences. Allowing for their being taken out of context, a few of the many instances of this device will serve nonetheless to illustrate the difficulties involved. Reuven is talking to Rachel:

"How do you feel?" I asked.
"Fragile," she said. Her face was faintly luminous in the darkness. "And raped."
I did not say anything. (37)

In the following instance, Reuven is talking to Danny:

"It's always easier to learn something than to use what you've learned."
I did not say anything.
"You're alone when you're learning. But you always use it on other people. It's different when there are other people involved."
I was quiet. (136)

In neither example is it clear that leaving Reuven mute works better than having him respond would. Indeed, one feels that the lack of response only serves to limit one's insight into the narrator and avoid dramatization. As first-person narrator and a central actor in the novel, Reuven's thoughts and attitudes are important enough to warrant dramatizing his responses in these instances as well as in others. However, he can express great distaste at someone like Rav Kalman and his attitudes or at Danny and his methods of treating Michael. There is no question of dishonesty on his part, his trustworthiness and sincerity make him a reliable if occasionally limited narrator.

The Promise is somewhat more oriented toward Reuven and his problems, with Potok creating in him a character who permits great empathy on the part of the reader. This is no small achievement given the rather esoteric nature of Reuven's goals and interests (ordination as a rabbi and logic) and the problems with which he is confronted in the novel (East European Jewish fundamentalism and a role as a go-between in relation to Michael Gordon, his parents, and Danny as therapist). However, Potok feels that there is a more even stress upon Reuven and Danny and that this created particular problems: "*The Promise* was especially difficult technically because it contained a double story (Reuven's and Danny's; *The Chosen* was really Danny's story) and a double climax (the ordination test and the isolation chamber scene), and the two had to be fused together organically from the very beginning."[16]

Potok succeeds in his characterization of Rav Kalman but not in that of a number of the minor characters, who, while demanding far less detail in their treatment, still require somewhat more individuation than they are given. One critic believes that "Although a host of figures appear in the novel, most of them, with the exception of Reuven's father and, less so, Rav Kalman, are stiff and phoney. The book's biggest phonies are Michael's aunt and his professorial parents. . . ."[17] I would not agree that Abraham Gordon is weakly characterized; however, Michael's aunt, uncle (always with a pipe), and mother certainly are.

The Chosen lacked any presentation of women. In *The Promise*, Potok includes three women and has Reuven show an awareness of the physical attractiveness of them all. Sarah Gordon is "a slender, fine-looking woman with oval features and auburn hair and gray eyes" (34); and Ruth Gordon is "a striking woman, tall, slender, lithe, with short chestnut hair and beautifully proportioned features . . ." (79). He later tells Rachel that Ruth Gordon "was one of the most beautiful women I had ever seen" (84). This goes some way to correct the imbalance in the earlier novel though it shows a bit of overkill in Reuven's reactions, especially as an early plot line concerns Reuven's romantic involvement with Rachel Gordon. It is as though Reuven has suddenly become aware of a different species around him and, politely of course, cannot take his eyes off it. The movement from virtually no women to all of these and the change in Reuven's awareness from *The Chosen* is somewhat blatant.

As an important minor character, Rachel receives a good deal of attention, some of it quite insightful as in the depiction of her love for Danny Saunders and the elucidation of her fears of what marrying a person still attached to the Hasidic tradition may mean to her and her future children. Less impressive is Potok's use of a "signal" to usher in a surprisingly large number of the encounters between Reuven and Rachel. This "signal" consists of ten or so references to James Joyce's *Ulysses,* on which Rachel is writing a paper on the "Ithaca" section. The allusions mostly comprise references to "James Joyce," "*Ulysses,*" and "Molly Bloom big with seed." The repetition of them is heavy-handed and intrusive, Potok making certain that we take note of them. In case we have missed the point, Reuven says to Rachel:

> "Tell me something, my lover of county fairs and James Joyce. Why did you pick the Ithaca section of *Ulysses* to do a paper on?"
> She looked at me curiously.
> "Was there a special reason?"
> "No," she murmured.
> "I reread it today. No special reason?"
> "No." There was a faint pink blush on her cheeks.
> "Danny is contagious," I said with a smile. "Or am I reading something into it that isn't really there?"
> She said nothing. But her eyes were moist. (249)

There is, of course, a "special reason" for Rachel's concentration on this section. The section stresses the importance of relationships, particularly the way in which Bloom and Stephen attempt to find a common ground in their differing responses to experience. These responses parallel Bloom's scientific temperament and Stephen's artistic one. Rachel must find points of common ground between Danny (psychology) and herself (literature). There are larger differences in their religious orientation. While these do not extend as far as Bloom's doubts as to whether or not he is a Jew, there is comparison possible in the way in which Bloom had treated with disrespect certain beliefs and practices.

As?

The prohibition of the use of fleshmeat and milk at one meal . . . :
the circumcision of male infants: the supernatural character of Judaic
scripture; the ineffability of the tetragrammaron: the sanctity of the
sabbath. [18]

Rachel, we are told, keeps the commandments; however, she
certainly is no Hasid, her parents (both professors) do not exhibit
any particular religiosity, and her uncle is the Reconstructionist
Abraham Gordon. Potok may be implying that Rachel's interest in
the "Ithaca" section of *Ulysses* is at least partially rooted in her
attempt to accommodate her religious practices and beliefs to Danny's. There is evidence within "Ithaca" that reconciliation of apparently dissimilar things is possible in the bringing together of
the Irish and Hebrew languages and in the ultimate vision of the
unity of the universe. The marriage of Rachel and Danny provides
an optimistic statement of the possibilities of reconciliation and
accommodation between different ideas that are, at base, unified in
their attachment to Judaism. The allusion is apt; however, the
method of its presentation is awkward.

There is a good deal of didacticism in both *The Chosen* and *The
Promise.* Potok is inherently a teacher, and this orientation often
makes its presence felt in his writing. One critic feels that *The
Promise* is based on "a condition (position? posture? stance?) that is
intellectual, like a theorem . . . and essentially static like a set of
postulates." [19] He goes on to point out that while it fails for him
as a novel because it is largely "exposition, not fiction," it does
"stand out as an intelligent discussion of, and many-sided approach
to, religiosity in 20th-century America." [20] This reaction is very
common in that many critics find themselves interested in and
favorably disposed toward the novel despite being critical of its
"sociological" approach or the "contrived" nature of its plot. The
harshest criticism, however, is reserved not for the novel's didacticism but for what one writer calls "the monochromed, mono-
rhythmed rhetoric, which gives a dubious unity to the novel . . . ;
people sound as if they were reading at each other rather than talking
naturally. . . ." [21] Unfortunately, this criticism is frequently war-
ranted, and it has been pointed out that "Reuven and Danny, both
presumably in their early twenties, are never guilty of such youthful

indiscretions as passion or rage. They can be depended on to react in one of five ways—'sadly,' 'mildly' 'thoughtfully,' 'quietly,' or 'solemnly'—although react is perhaps the wrong word since they confine themselves strictly to speech."[22] This is not entirely fair, as passion there is; however, it is muted by the stress upon words instead of action. Nonetheless, words, and what lies behind them, can provide both passion and rage, as is the case in many instances in *The Promise.*

As in *The Chosen,* the appeal of *The Promise* lies in its sincerity. Potok's didacticism is not the only thing that comes through. He believes in his people, and the characterizations, though frequently leaving more to be desired, are sufficient to permit us as readers to believe in them as well. They stand for a set of values which are ultimately ethical and righteous, and the working out of the conflicts caused by strongly held beliefs is often gripping and always moving. A novel of ideas, such as *The Promise,* can easily lapse into a philosophical essay which diverges too greatly from the novel as an art form. It need not do so, as one master of the form—Saul Bellow— observes: "Among modern novelists the bravest have taken the risk of teaching and have not been afraid of using the terms of religion, science, philosophy, and politics. Only they have been prepared to admit the strongest possible arguments against their own positions. . . . This, I think, is the greatest achievement possible in a novel of ideas. It becomes art when the views most opposite to the author's own are allowed to exist in full strength. Without this a novel of ideas is mere self-indulgence, and didacticism is simply axe-grinding."[23]

Bellow's points are directly applicable to *The Promise.* As mentioned, Potok is certainly a teacher; he presents specific information concerning Jewish lore, yeshiva curricula, and theological stances. In addition, he illustrates Bellow's view that arguments with which the author disagrees should receive full treatment. While Potok would not personally accept Rav Kalman's extreme "right wing" views, it is doubtful whether he would fully accept Abraham Gordon's extreme "left wing" ones either. David Malter and Reuven are closest to him in their ideas of Judaism. This does not prevent him from giving both Rav Kalman's and Abraham Gordon's ideas full exposure. Indeed, he seems to revel in the thrust and parry of the debate which the three sincerely held interpretations of Judaism engender.

In *The Promise,* Potok has taken a complex set of ideas and managed to fashion a fascinating tale out of them. This is an admirable achievement. Faults there are, but as Lillian Elkin writes: "Despite the flaws of characterization and point of view, *The Promise* is a major achievement. It portrays the painful struggle between tradition and the modern spirit with rare understanding of both. . . . Even though our sympathies are with Abraham Gordon, David and Reuven Malter, we can understand Rav Kalman and the remnants of a European world destroyed twenty-five years ago. This is possible because Chaim Potock [*sic*] writes with his heart and his head, avoiding a simple conclusion for a complex situation."[24] Both the situation and the main characters remain with us.

Chapter Four
My Name Is Asher Lev
Judaism and the Visual Arts

My Name Is Asher Lev concerns a clash between the secular and Orthodox Jewish cultures. Asher Lev is born with a gift: he is an artist of great talent. As a child he finds that he loves to draw and begins to do it to the point where it becomes more than merely a pastime. He begins to see the world around him through an artist's eyes, in terms of form and color. His interest in art becomes an obsession which takes precedence over his religious responsibilities and secular school work.

Far from this artistic gift being valued by his parents and community, it is seen as un-Jewish and a threat to his religion. Asher's father, Aryeh Lev ("Aryeh" means lion), cannot understand or appreciate it and puts intense pressure on his son to stop his drawing and painting and concentrate upon his studies of the Bible, Talmud, and other school subjects. Since Aryeh "travels for the Rebbe," tries to spread the particular type of Hasidism in which he believes (called "Ladover," it is modeled on Lubavitch Hasidism), it is all the more galling to him that his son slights his religious education for something in which neither the community nor he places any value. When Asher's art leads him to paint nudes and crucifixions, the conflict between father and son reaches great intensity.

Recognizing that the gift cannot be stifled, the Rebbe tries to harness it for the community by arranging for a famous Jewish artist, Jacob Kahn, to guide Asher. This occurs at the significant age of thirteen, when Asher is to take on the full religious responsibilities of a Jewish male. Kahn's devotion to art is such, however, that Asher learns to place it above almost anything. In Kahn's estimation, art is a religious calling to which all other pursuits and values must take second place. The result of this clash of ideas is that in order to be true to his art, Asher must disregard certain community values. A point is reached where the difference in the demands of the two areas—art and community—is so great that

Asher must choose one or the other. The Rebbe tells him that he must leave the community to avoid hurting people, as he had with his famous painting *The Brooklyn Crucifixion*. Asher goes to Paris to live, but it is implied that he will retain his ties to Judaism.

There is much in *My Name Is Asher Lev* that relates to Chaim Potok's own experiences. As a teenager he painted and sketched but found that his father did not like it: "He thought it was a terrible waste of time,"[1] Potok has said. He gave up painting for writing, which he had been doing since he was fourteen years old, in order to avoid "conflicts" with the Jewish tradition. However, he says that "The writing simply delayed it for a while. Asher Lev was the metaphor for the problems of the writer."[2]

Writer or painter, it did not matter since both vocations called for adherence to the dictates of art. In depicting the problems of the painter, Potok could depict the problems of any artist trying to reconcile the demands of art with those of an ancient religious tradition. He has recalled being told to see his Talmud teacher, who had heard that he was writing in his spare time. The teacher felt that writing fiction "was alien to the essential nature of the Jewish tradition. And not alien in an innocent way but alien in a crucial way. . . . It was potentially a threat to the Jewish value system. That was the beginning for me of a very lengthy bad time with this rabbi and all the other rabbis that I had all through my remaining years in high school and college."[3] It is telling that Potok goes on to say that this teacher's view of the danger of art to the Jewish tradition proved to be right. This danger did not drive Potok away from Judaism; however, it did make it impossible for him to remain attached to the brand of fundamentalism in which he had been raised, and he has spoken of that break as "irrevocable."[4]

Potok presents the basic conflict of the novel as a clash of loves and responsibilities. Again, this parallels his own experiences:

By the time I was about twenty I found myself the inheritor of two utterly antithetical ultimate commitments. The enterprise we call modern literature tells you to take no human institution as intrinsically sacred, no human act as intrinsically incapable of being poked into by the pen of the writer. No thought, feeling, no sensibility is so sacred that it cannot be tapped or explored and revealed. And the religious tradition that I inherited said to me that there are things that are intrinsically sacred, that there is a certain stance that one should take about the universe. And I loved that tradition. I didn't want to break with it.[5]

The result of this clash of "commitments" was that Potok came to feel that "Any kind of Orthodoxy and serious art are at best gentle adversaries and at worst mortal enemies. It is not the purpose of art to embellish orthodoxies. . . . Orthodox Jewish life became for me a symbol of the collapse of art."[6] The ultimate irreconcilability of art and Jewish Orthodoxy is at the center of *My Name Is Asher Lev*.

The novel begins with an epigraph, Picasso's statement that "art is a lie which makes us realize the truth."[7] Immediately we must consider what sort of truth can emerge from a lie? This "truth" is an aesthetic one, a truth to an individual artist's perception of reality. Numerous individuals may find that it bears no relation to their own view of reality and may consider it false. It will be particularly difficult to accept if an external set of values is superimposed upon the art form making certain demands other than the purely aesthetic. Judaism makes numerous demands which have no aesthetic base at all; indeed, the religion is suspicious of purely aesthetic motives: "The Jew's aesthetics are in the service of morality, the service of man and the service of the commandments. But the aesthetics of Asher Lev are just aesthetics for the sake of beauty itself, for the sake of enhancing the world so that it becomes a prettier place to live in."[8] While we see Asher Lev becoming more and more concerned with depicting the world as harsh and not pretty, Potok's point is that aesthetic considerations are all important.

Asher visits a Jewish museum: "I saw Torah crowns, Torah pointers, Torah covers, spice boxes, illuminated manuscripts. Some were fine pieces of work. But there was no art. It was all crafts and unmoving. I felt vaguely betrayed" (281). Asher's inability to find within the Jewish tradition an aesthetic concern explains why he has such difficulty with his father, who is a representative of that tradition.

Jacob Kahn explains to Asher that Aryeh's education did not in any way prepare him for an appreciation of art, quite the opposite: "Why should your father understand painting? From a yeshiva education you get a case of aesthetic blindness. . . . He will appreciate a pretty calendar picture of Abraham and the angels or Rebecca at the well. But he would not want his son to dedicate his life to making such pictures. He certainly would not want his son to dedicate his life to making the kind of pictures his son is actually making" (296–97). His two degrees in political science and his long stays in Europe have not made any difference to his artistic appreciation, and Kahn observes that numerous people in eminent positions are similarly incapable of appreciating art.

Aryeh Lev places moral evaluations upon an area about which he knows nothing and for which his tradition has not prepared him. His suspicion of the artistic process reflects a suspicion within the Jewish tradition for those areas of the psyche which are difficult to control. Potok states that for Halachic Judaism "those elements of man which are connected to the unconscious or sub-conscious must be carefully controlled. . . . This tight control is the antithesis to the artistic enterprise, which is plugged directly into this libidinous element of the human being."[9] When he tries to explain the artist's view of the world to his father, a point is reached where Asher must repeat Jacob Kahn's accusation:

"An interesting concept. Aesthetic blindness. And what about moral blindness, Asher?"
"I'm not hurting anybody, Papa."
"One day you will, Asher. This will lead you to the sitra achra."
"No."
"Asher, if you had a choice between aesthetic blindness and moral blindness, which would you choose?"
I said nothing.
"I'm warning you, Asher. One day you'll hurt someone with this kind of attitude. And then you'll be doing the work of the sitra achra." (304–5)

Asher's silence to his father's question is most telling. Despite his ignorance of art, Aryeh's instincts are sound: it is a threat to the Jewish tradition and to what he understands as morality within that tradition. When Potok was asked whether one can have art without morality, he answered that "There's a good case for art as delectation, for the sheer joy of a pure aesthetic experience."[10] This would be Asher's answer as well.

Resistance to art and the artist within the Jewish tradition has a historical source. Potok has explained this resistance thus: "In the ancient world all art was inextricably linked with paganism, with the gods—you made images of the gods and you wrote dramas for the gods. The Jew, the Israelite, came into the world with an alternative reading of reality. His world was not bound by the nature deities and he loathed the image-making activity of man. . . . Once the image-making became stripped of its relationship to the gods, the Jew began to enter that arena of creativity as well. . . ."[11] The Israelites turned from three-dimensional image-making to words as the basis of their creativity. Aryeh Lev tells Asher that he would understand if he possessed genius in mathematics or writing, but "a genius in drawing is foolishness . . ." (141). Of course, a "genius in writing" might well present similar or worse problems for Aryeh; that he thinks he would understand that better than genius in the pictorial arts, only shows how little comprehension he has of the nature of the artistic vision.

Traditionally, "Scholarship, or charity, was the highest form of service. It was more meritorious to provide bread for the poor, or books for the student, than adornments for the synagogue. The centrality of cult objects, which was almost fundamental to Christianity and was thus responsible for the finest artistic achievements of the Middle Ages, was hence absent in Judaism. Jewish life gained in warmth what the synagogue lost in artistic beauty."[12] Aside from purely communal reasons, which I shall be considering shortly, Jewish history and the traditions which developed out of it did not favor a positive response to the pictorial or plastic arts. However, there was never an outright ban upon their practice, the major result of the negative attitudes in which they were held being that the status of the artist within Orthodox Jewish society remained low.

It is often observed that the root cause of Jewish resistance to art throughout the centuries is biblical. The second commandment states that "Thou shalt not make unto thee a graven image, nor any manner of likeness, of any thing that is in the heaven above, or that is in the earth beneath, or that is in the water under the earth; thou shalt not bow down unto them, nor serve them . . ." (Exodus 20:4–5). This prohibition is restated and made even more specific later in the Hebrew Bible when the Israelites are told by God, through Moses, that to avoid the possibility of them worshipping an image—since they have never seen an image of the Lord—they are prohibited from making "a graven image, even the form of any figure, the likeness of male or female, the likeness of any beast that is on the earth, the likeness of any winged fowl that flieth in the heaven, the likeness of any thing that creepeth on the ground, the likeness of any fish that is in the water under the earth . . ." (Deuteronomy 4:16–18). Dr. J. H. Hertz, the late chief rabbi of the British Empire, has stated that the second commandment "forbids the worship of the One God in the wrong way. Judaism alone, from the very beginning, taught that God was a Spirit; and made it an unpardonable sin to worship God under any external form that human hands can fashion. No doubt this law hindered the free development of plastic arts in ancient Israel; but it was of incalculable importance for the purity of the conception of God."[13]

The important point here is that both the second commandment and the reference in Deuteronomy stress avoidance of idolatry, and the spiritual nature of God. It was not that pictorial or three-dimensional representations of animals, objects, or man himself were inherently evil; it was that the Israelites were to be a people who followed a new god who, unlike the gods of the surrounding peoples, could not be represented or worshipped in the form of an idol. Indeed, it was not the case that the biblical prohibitions led to a uniform abhorrence of images. In considering the effects of the biblical passages cited upon Jewish attitudes toward representational art, Cecil Roth states:

Whether the passages in question were intended as outright prohibition of the representation of any human or animal form in any circumstances is questionable. But what is certain is that it was not always so interpreted, even among Jews of the most rigid and unswerving loyalty. Indeed the Pentateuchal code itself, with its detailed instructions regarding the Cherubim which were to be placed in the Ark, suggests the logical conclusion that the stern negative of the Ten Commandments was intended to be read in conjunction with the following verse: "Thou shalt not bow down to them and shalt not serve them"—that is, that no image must be made for the purpose of worship, either as representing or as substituting the Divinity.

In all Jewish history, attitudes and interpretations varied from land to land and from generation to generation. . . . Sometimes men went to the other extreme, and great latitude was shown, human figures being incorporated freely even in objects associated with Divine worship.[14]

He goes on to point out that the only relative consistency in approach of Jewish communities through the centuries has been in regard to busts and statues of human beings, which did not begin to appear in any great number until the seventeenth or eighteenth centuries. Even in relation to these, however, there were earlier exceptions. Thus, generalizations are impossible to make.

The Rebbe understands this. He tells Asher:

"A life should be lived for the sake of heaven. One man is not better than another because he is a doctor while the other is a shoemaker. One man is not better than another because he is a lawyer while the other is a painter. A life is measured by how it is lived for the sake of heaven. Do you understand me, Asher Lev?"

"Yes, Rebbe."

"But there are those who do not understand this."

I was quiet.

"There are those you love and who love you who do not accept this." (195)

The Rebbe has a much broader view than others in the community, particularly Aryeh Lev whose attitude toward art is tacitly criticized. Clearly the Rebbe would not speak as he does if he felt that painting was anathema to Judaism. What is important is the motivation behind it, the purpose for which it is done. This is not to say that the Rebbe accepts or understands the artistic impulse. He asks Jacob Kahn to keep Asher from "evil ways." Kahn tells Asher: "I do not know what evil is when it comes to art. I only know what is good art and what is bad art. Those were my words to the Rebbe. The Rebbe trusts me and will rely on my honest heart. . . . I will not teach you on the basis of that trust. Artists should not be trusted. If an artist is not deceitful every so often in the cause of his art then he is a poor artist. Those were my remarks to the Rebbe. Still, he trusts me" (216).

The Rebbe is trying to save Asher for the Jewish community. He knows that Asher's gift will not go away; if possible, it must be channeled into the service of Judaism. His trust of Jacob Kahn, given what Kahn has said to him, is only explicable in terms of a realization that there is no other way. The focus of attention must now move from the aesthetic and historical aspects to the communal ones, for it is in relation to the community that Asher Lev has many of his greatest problems.

The Individual and the Community

Although there have been many great Jews from biblical times to the present day, Judaism places more stress upon the Jewish people than upon the individual. The survival of the people with whom God made His covenant is of central importance in Jewish tradition. Asher Lev's problem stems from the fact that he reaches a point where, like Danny Saunders, he places more stress upon his own personal fulfillment than upon the furtherance of the goals of the Jewish community. The mashpia, who is responsible for both the development of the souls of the young as well as teaching the doctrines of Ladover Hasidism, tells Asher of the many people in the community who have been born with "gifts." He then says that "one does not always give in to a gift. One does with a life what is precious not only to one's own self but to one's own people. That is the way our people live, Asherel. . . . The gift causes you to think only of yourself and your own feelings. No one would care if these were normal times, Asherel. We do not interpret the second commandment the way others do" (133). Asher's reaction, quite reasonably, is that times have never been "normal" for Jews. It must also be said that even if times were comparatively normal, people would be unlikely to accept Asher's painting with as much equanimity as the mashpia implies.

The stifling of individual abilities for the general good may be viewed as admirable selflessness or unfortunate waste. Asher wonders: "What is he telling me. To stifle my gift? Does he also believe the gift is from the Other Side? Then it should be stifled even in normal times; what does it have to do with the Jewish people? And if it's not from the Other Side, if it's from the Ribbono Shel Olom, why is it less important than what Papa is doing?" (133). As we have seen, these "theological" questions are particularly difficult to answer because of the ambiguousness of the Orthodox Jewish reaction to artistic endeavor. Asher's questioning what art has to do with the Jewish people heightens our realization of his inability to grasp what the community is telling him. The point is that art has nothing to do with the Jewish community—that is the problem.

In addition to the resistance of the community to Asher's interests on traditional grounds, there is a more basic reason for their inability to accept his needs; his stress upon the importance of an individual vision threatens the cohesiveness of communal values. While it possesses a clear religious nature, the Jewish community presented in the novel shares elements with all minority groups, religious or not. The most important element so far as community survival is concerned is conformity to accepted rules and attitudes. Add to this the insecure nature of most minority communities and, perhaps, of Jewish ones in particular, and it is not surprising that Asher's stress upon individual above group needs is seen as dangerous. This is reflected in the reactions of major authority figures (the mashpia, Aryeh Lev) and more ordinary members of the community (Asher's Hebrew teacher, Uncle Yitzchok, Yudel Krinsky, Mrs. Rackover, and the pupils in Asher's class). The Rebbe, as we have seen, has a more complex understanding of Asher's problem, trying unsuccessfully to channel his gift into areas that may serve the community.

The one character within the group apart from the Rebbe who has a sympathetic understanding of Asher's needs is his mother. After the death of her brother, Rivkeh feels the need to complete his work and gains the Rebbe's permission to go to college to pursue studies in Russian language and history. No other women are presented in the novel who are permitted to engage in activities in the world, which would normally be considered acceptable only for men. She understands what it means to be driven to fulfill a task. It is not altogether surprising, therefore, that despite her husband's constant and strong resistance to Asher's painting, she takes him to the museum and, difficult though it is for her, accompanies him when he views nudes and crucifixions. She buys him oil paints and gives him money to buy his own. Potok depicts her position between husband and son with great sensitivity. Her grave doubts concerning Asher's painting, and the sort of paintings which he must study, are overcome by her understanding of his desperate need to express himself, which parallels her need to complete her brother's work. It is Rivkeh's position between husband and son that will inscribe itself upon Asher's consciousness and lead to the creation of his greatest paintings. These paintings will lead to his forced departure from the community.

The Jewish group in the novel comprises both the local Brooklyn one and the Jewish people worldwide. It is not only the local community against which Asher must set his individuality but against the moral pressures exerted by Jews in Europe and Russia. The mashpia tells Asher of the Rebbe's father: "All the Jewish people are one body and one soul, he believed. If one part of the body hurts, the entire body hurts—and the entire body must come to the help of the part that hurts. . . . Asherel, your father also sees the Jewish people as one body and one soul. When a head hurts in the Ukraine, your father suffers in Brooklyn. When Jews cannot study Torah in Kiev, your father cannot sit still in Brooklyn" (132). Indeed, Aryeh tells Asher of his belief in the importance of making "passageways" to God and Judaism for the Jews of Russia. Thus,

Asher's growing desire for fulfillment of individual non-Jewish needs is set against the preservation of the Jewish people as a whole and the alleviation of real suffering. His breakdown before the mashpia concerning whether or not he will go to Vienna with his parents reflects these pressures. Ultimately, the gift does make him selfish, and his fear of losing it overrides all other considerations. As Warren True observes: "Even though the result of his choices will be exile, he fears the darkness of his suppression more . . . . The consequences of choosing one's personal and aesthetic course over that dictated by family, nation, and religion is alienation from all three."[15] Although Asher tells us that he remains an observant Jew, he is forced to leave the Brooklyn community and will spend his life engaged in an activity which at best places him in an ambiguous position in relation to the Jewish tradition.

Halfway through the novel Asher can still respond to Jacob Kahn's question of whom he feels responsible to with:

"All Jews are responsible one for the other," I said quoting the statement from the Talmud my father had years ago quoted to me.

"As an artist you are responsible to Jews?" He seemed angry. "Listen to me, Asher Lev. As an artist you are responsible to no one and to nothing, except your self and to the truth as you see it. Do you understand? An artist is responsible to art. Anything else is propoganda" (218)

In order for Asher to achieve the highest level of artistic success, he must move beyond community and take on a new loyalty. The lives of his father and mother are ruled, and given meaning, by the Rebbe, who has told Aryeh what degrees to obtain and has to be consulted before Rivkeh can go to college. The Rebbe has also directed Aryeh's travels and those of Rivkeh's brother; he has told the Lev family to move to Vienna. The Rebbe has ordered Asher to study French, which he reluctantly accepts, and Russian, which he does not. In his refusal to study Russian, Asher has rejected the role that his parents accept and that, in the context of the Ladover community, equates with responsibility to Jews. The Rebbe's attempts to glimpse Asher's future, to take over his life's decisions for him as he has for his parents, cannot succeed if Asher is to be a great artist. He tells him that "Seeds must be sown everywhere. Only some will bear fruit. . . . I give you my blessings for greatness in the world of art and greatness in the world of your people" (285).

Unfortunately, Asher cannot sow seeds as his father has and cannot be great in both the worlds of art and of his people.

The result of this clash of values becomes more and more predictable as the novel progresses. Despite the Rebbe's attempts to harness Asher's gift for the Jewish people and the genuine warmth with which Asher is welcomed back into the community upon his return from Europe, his exhibition of the crucifixion paintings signal his final break with the Brooklyn community. The Rebbe is, perhaps, too understanding here, Jacob Kahn's having explained the importance of Christian models to an artist notwithstanding. He must send Asher away not for doctrinal reasons but human ones: "You are too close here to people you love. You are hurting them and making them angry. They are good people. They do not understand you" (266). The implication is that Asher will live in Paris, marry a member of the Ladover community there, and continue as both an artist and a Jew. Potok convinces us of the necessity for the break to occur but stops short of removing Asher from observance of the commandments and attachment to Ladover Hasidism. We might have been more convinced if the novel had followed the course toward which it was inexorably moving: Asher's break with both the Brooklyn community and Hasidism, if not with Orthodox Judaism itself. A justification within the novel for his continuing attachment to Ladover Hasidism is presented through Asher's mythic ancestor, who also heightens the theme of ancestors, fathers, and sons.

Ancestors and Fathers

Although the novel is set in a particular time and place, Potok makes us aware of the influence of events centuries past. Asher must live with the awareness of the Jewish tradition even at night, when his "mythic ancestor" comes to him in dreams and nightmares, reproaching him for any deviation through his art from accepted, traditional Jewish norms. His family ancestry is so weighted with Jewish history that Asher's rebellion is seen in terms of increasingly widening circles: from the Brooklyn community to the worldwide Jewish one to the Jewish tradition as exemplified by his own family's activities through the centuries. Like Danny Saunders in *The Chosen* Asher has inherited a responsibility he feels he cannot fulfill; however, the tale develops to a point where an accommodation between Asher and his ancestor can occur.

The mythic ancestor had made himself wealthy as an estate manager for a Russian nobleman. The noble, who also became wealthy as a result of the ancestor's skill, burned down a village while drunk, killing several serfs. Later in life, the mythic ancestor began to travel to, as Aryeh Lev states, "do good deeds and bring the Master of the Universe into the world . . ." (4). This tradition is one that has been carried on in the Lev family ever since and which Asher seems in the process of breaking. It is directly related to the theme of completion, which plays a central role in the motivations of Asher's parents. Great moral weight is placed upon the necessity of completing tasks begun, particularly those done for Judaism and the Master of the Universe. Aryeh Lev is obsessed with creating yeshivas in Europe and helping Jews in the Soviet Union escape. He does these things to complete the tasks begun by his ancestors. Similarly, Rivkeh Lev decides that she must complete her brother's work. He died while on a mission for the Rebbe, and by studying Russian language and culture she hopes to be able to help her husband in his work and so justify her brother's death.

Asher wonders whether in making the nobleman wealthy, his mythic ancestor did not in some way share the blame for the peasants whom he murdered? He wonders whether "the journeys of that mythic ancestor might have been born in the memories of screams and burning flesh. A balance had to be given the world; the demonic had to be reshaped into meaning. Had a dream-haunted Jew spent the rest of his life sculpting form out of the horror of his private night?" (323). Asher begins to see the whole pattern of traveling of his forebears as based upon a need for atonement. The need to balance evil, the "demonic," has been the cause of the incessant traveling not only of his ancestors but of his father as well. One of the primary reasons for his father's strident resistance to his son's passion for art may well be Aryeh's realization that Asher is not only standing outside the Jewish tradition as he sees it but is breaking with the Lev family's traditional way of expressing that tradition. Indeed, Asher wonders whether he had with his "need to give meaning to paper and canvas rather than to people and events, interrupted an act of eternal atonement?" (325). A need for completion combined with a possible sense of responsibility for a past wrong has driven the Levs throughout the centuries—until Asher.

In order to resolve the problem, Asher must be able to combine family traditions in an acceptable manner. This he does succeed in doing to a point, although his interpretation of his situation is not shared by his father. One critic observed that the mythic ancestor is a device that Aryeh and Rivkeh use to explain the family tradition of traveling. Although Asher originally accepts his parents' view, he must change his interpretation since it does not permit him to use his gift: "Instead he develops his own interpretation of the myth as he develops his art and identity, and the novel becomes 'a long session in demythology.' Because Asher has never seen his great-great-great-grandfather, his perception of the mythic ancestor reflects his own attitude towards the myth, and the nature of his dreams therefore changes as his attitude changes."[16]

Asher's guilt feelings can be seen through his dreams. When he hurts his mother through his refusal to go to Europe with her and his father or when he paints Pietàs while in Florence, his mythic ancestor comes to him in the form of nightmares, "dark-bearded and dark-visaged, thundering his rage" (316). However, after copying both Michelangelo's *Pietà* and his *David,* the mythic ancestor comes to Asher "less thunderous than he had ever been before and did not wake me from my sleep" (313), the implication being that the time spent on the *David* is acceptable. There is a slow development, an integration, of the demands of the mythic ancestor into Asher's conception of the basic nature of his artistic vision; that is, since he cannot relinquish the need to express his artistic vision, Asher justifies, rationalizes if you will, the practice of his art with the inescapable demands of his ancestor for responsibility to the Jewish tradition.

He finds that his ancestor is presenting him with ways in which he can use his art to serve the Jewish people and mankind. Toward the end of the novel, he dreams that his ancestor tells him to "Come with me, my precious Asher. You and I will walk together now through the centuries, each of us for our separate deeds that unbalanced the world" (347). The ancestor places his own "sin" in permitting the death-dealing noble to become wealthy on a par with Asher's "sin" of choosing art over tradition. Both can use their actions for positive purposes: to show the pain in the world and try to counter evil with good. The ancestor advises Asher to become a great painter, as "that will be the only justification for all the pain you will cause. . . . Now journey with me, my Asher. Paint the anguish of all the world. Let people see the pain. But create your own molds and your own play of forms for the pain" (367–68).

Sam Sutherland has pointed out that the advice that Asher imagines his ancestor is giving him here was also given to him by Jacob Kahn, who felt that the only way for Asher to justify the pain that he would cause would be for him to become a great artist: "This merging of the two insights shows that Asher has stripped the myth away from the truth it tried to represent, and that he can now directly perceive his relationship with God. No longer must he follow the mythic tradition of journeying, but he can now serve God and give balance to the universe through his own play of forms . . . , his own means of expression: art."[17]

Asher manages to get what he wants: art plus a place within the tradition. This, however, is not acceptable to his father, who sees his son's early interest in drawing and painting as foolishness and a waste of time and his later obsession with it as evil and a desecration. Aryeh Lev is the modern representative of the mythic ancestor without Asher's "revisionism." His attachment to his inherited role remains unchanged. He would not be capable of understanding the relationship with the tradition which Asher is able to make. One critic thinks that "it is in the very process of becoming an established part of the alien tradition of art that we see him becoming at last his father's son and the inheritor of Jewish tradition."[18] In the sense that Asher must come to grips with both the artistic and Jewish traditions, struggling to find a point of convergence between the two because of his love for both, one may say that he remains a moral individual who possesses a sense of responsibility. He cannot, however, be called "his father's son,"[19] even though Potok ends the novel with Rivkeh repeating the phrase "Have a safe journey" (369).

His journey will be different from that of his father and, despite the sense of guilt his art creates in him, his "atonement" is different from that of his mythic ancestor. Asher's journey is not selfless, as is his father's, nor do his feelings of guilt at what he has done to people in the community and to his parents cause him to give up his art and so truly atone for his "sins." His remaining an observant Jew comes as a surprise despite his telling us that after a heavy snowfall he, symbolically, "walked carefully in paths made by others who had gone before me" (336); these "others" could be artists and not religious Jews. He accepts that he will continue to cause pain to others because of his art whose nature is both demonic and divine, as he recognizes himself to be. A reconciliation of Asher's gift and his mythic ancestor's demands must be seen as illusory, except, that is, to Asher himself whose creativity extends to an ability to reform myths to suit his own urgent needs.

Artistic and Stylistic Development

In this section I shall show how the marked improvement in Potok's literary technique has enabled him to present a convincing portrayal of the development of Asher Lev as an artist. With this novel, Potok has taken a step forward in the subtlety and nuance of his writing, having eliminated many of the flaws of his previous works. Like *The Chosen* and *The Promise, My Name Is Asher Lev* is presented through a first-person narrator who is also a central character. Unlike the second novel, however, it is told in long-term retrospect, the narrator looking back over his life and describing his development as an artist from the age of four. After a three-page description of his present negative reputation among religious Jews and Christians and a summary of his Jewish ancestry, Asher moves to his childhood. The narrative traces his life chronologically until it arrives again at the present day. One critic points out the unity that Potok achieves in the novel because of the fact that "The content of Asher's narrative is similar: it is about how the past reaches into the present until it becomes the present."[20] As we have seen, the past is crucial to the novel's themes: it is also of central importance to its structure, Asher's development as both an artist and an individual being seen in relation to the pressures placed upon him by his own reactions to his past (his mythical ancestor) and the community's interpretation of what the Jewish past demands. The constant infusion of the past into the present provides an almost Faulknerian effect; the present cannot be seen in isolation from the past but can only develop in relation to it. One can also see the influence of James Joyce, in particular *A Portrait of the Artist as a Young Man,* on Potok's style and themes, at least one critic feeling that this influence is overwhelming.[21]

In a review of Saul Bellow's novel, *The Dean's December,* Potok wrote: "Listen to the voices. Forgive the occasional woodenness; it is found in any writer working in nondramatic situations where words are without the impetus of movement. Marvelous things happen in this book as people talk. Ideas are exchanged, reformulated, tested, cast away, taken up. Souls are bared. There are anger, mockery, pain, bewilderment, warmth, love—all in the talk, high serious sober talk."[22] This passage can be viewed as a comment both upon Bellow's style and Potok's own. The three novels thus far discussed have all relied heavily upon ideas—sometimes in action, sometimes not. Potok has frequently been accused of writing dialogue that is wooden, which does not set his ideas in action. In making a plea for the ignoring of "occasional woodenness" in Bellow's novel, one can see a plea for a similar indulgence to be given to his own work. Novelists of ideas, which both Potok and Bellow are, do have the problem of creating novels that are more than tracts or polemics (something that Bellow largely fails to do in *Mr. Sammler's Planet,* for instance). However, whereas Bellow has created a muscular dialogue in most of his novels, one containing both richness and humor, Potok has not managed to do the same and has been consistently criticized on this account.

One reaction to *My Name Is Asher Lev* sums up the negative criticism of its dialogue, the critic wishing that "Mr. Potok could have gotten away from that primerlike style of his. The succession of simple declarative sentences becomes cloying and sweet, the dialogue sticky. It is impossible, for example, to distinguish one voice from another. Everyone talks the same way and every speech is full of clotted wisdom."[23] We have read similar criticisms of the previous two novels. Nonetheless, this particular critic likes the book, stating that Potok "has manipulated the twin ideas of artistic fulfillment and community loyalty with a deftness that sometimes disguises the chances he took."[24] This interpretation is correct, Potok transcending a weakness of dialogue with ideas and a plot that make for a fascinating and moving work. It is the narrative and descriptive passages that raise this novel above the previous two stylistically. While it is difficult to "Listen to the voices" here because the dialogue is not rendered effectively enough, one can listen to Asher's narration and descriptions with the greatest interest and pleasure.

Early in the novel, Asher describes the way in which his perception of the world around him begins to take on increasing visual depth: "It was a steady rain and it fell with soft sounds against the stone and the street. After a while, I watched from inside the rain and no longer knew I was watching. . . . The asphalt glittered darkly in the rain. The rain cut through the circles of light around the tops of the lamp-posts, cold silvery diagonals against the warm

yellow-white arcs of brightness. The street seemed to be crying"
(45). Asher literally sees the world differently from those around
him, Potok's use of imagery and personification effectively conveying
the uniqueness of his vision.

The vision becomes an integral part of Asher's way of responding
to people and emotions. When his mother asks him if he is drawing
pretty things, Asher says, "I was drawing twisted shapes, swirling
forms, in blacks and reds and grays" (17), his feelings toward his
world in the midst of his mother's illness being reflected in his
pictures. Similarly Potok depicts Asher's artistic growth and his
ability to empathize with certain people through his drawing. For
instance, he sees his understanding uncle's suits as light not dark
blue and tries to discover which colors best express cold and dark
because of his sympathy with Yudel Krinsky, the man whose escape
from Russia his father made possible. Asher finds that art gives him
a greater understanding of situations that would otherwise be closed
to him. Also, his emotional response to human suffering is made
possible because of his artistic gift:

I could not imagine what it was like to live in ice and darkness. I put my
hands over my eyes. There was his face very clearly; not truly his face,
but the way I felt about his face. I drew his face inside my head. I went
to my desk and on a piece of blank white paper drew how I felt about his
face. . . . Now there was ice and darkness inside me. I could feel the cold
darkness moving slowly inside me. I could feel our darkness. It seemed
to me then that we were brothers, he and I, that we both knew lands of
ice and darkness. His had been in the past; mine was within me. Yes, we
were brothers, he and I, and I felt closer to him at that moment than to
any other human being in all the world. (41)

What Potok has skillfully shown here is a movement from ignorance to understanding through art. Asher begins by being unable
to grasp what eleven years in Siberia actually mean. His attempts
to transform that fact into artistic form actualizes the experience for
him. Yudel Krinsky's face changes under Asher's contemplation of
it becoming his own creation. Through a strong use of imagery and
metaphor, Potok transforms what has been abstract concepts to
Asher ("ice and darkness") into human sympathy and identity ("we
were brothers"). Thus the artistic process is seen as not a totally
selfish one but something that has the power to enhance one's
response to human emotions and feelings.

Potok combines descriptions of the setting and of other characters with a sense of Asher's developing artist's eye. The choice of first-person narration permits him to show the world of the novel through Asher's eyes, and, as we have seen, these eyes see the world in a particular way. A simple description of a room becomes an exercise in imagistic seeing when Asher describes it, and he says that "Sometimes my eyes would hurt after a day of watching" (33).

Potok convincingly describes an almost physiological change in Asher's sight, and his fright at this change is most effectively conveyed. An examination by an eye doctor shows nothing wrong with his eyes; one by a psychiatrist leaves his mother "subdued," the strain of the conflict taking its toll on Asher. The "gift" appears to be taking over Asher's free will, leaving him powerless to control it. When Potok describes him as being able to "feel with my eyes" (108), this personification implies both artistic feeling and, as we have seen, feeling in the sense of human empathy and sympathy. In addition, there is a certain distancing of the narrator from the action in his stating that he could feel his eyes moving in a certain manner and thinks that he can now see with "another pair of eyes . . ." (108). These descriptions of uncontrollable changes brought to bear upon Asher Lev heighten the sense of his powerlessness. This, in turn, bolsters the conflict at the root of the novel causing the reader to view the protagonist not in terms of one selfishly pursuing a desired course of action but of someone who is driven by forces beyond his control. Despite the way in which Asher hurts his family and community, we can still see him as being more a victim of his gift than its initiator.

His desperation is depicted in graphic terms when he is asked by the mashpia to draw some pictures for him. Asher draws people and scenes from his neighborhood, becoming increasingly carried away by the task: "I drew until the point of the pencil was gone; then I tore at the wood with my fingernails to get to the lead. . . . Then I no longer knew what I was drawing. . . . I hated what I had drawn in that sketchbook" (137–38). It is noteworthy that despite the fact that Asher despises them, the drawings he has produced are good enough to impress Jacob Kahn sufficiently so that he is willing to become Asher's teacher. The gift has taken him over, and it is difficult for him to draw badly. Later on Asher will tell his father that he cannot help drawing; he is not in control. Aryeh's

angry rejoinder that Asher must fight against it because it is evil
is not effective—the demands of the gift are too strong.

Even as a child Asher is aware of certain moral implications in
the relationship between art and the world. He draws spots of
perspiration on his mother's face with great care instead of drawing
pretty flowers, and during her illness he despairs that his drawings
do not help to make the world a better place. He draws his con-
valescing mother, still gaunt, and "drained of substance" and tells
his father that "I wanted to draw the light and the dark . . ." (35).
For a time he manages to stop drawing completely because of a
feeling that "To draw, to make lines and shapes on pieces of paper,
was a futile indulgence in the face of such immutable darkness, a
foolishness I would certainly leave behind . . ." (49). Some of this
feeling of the futility of drawing comes from the constant pressure
of Aryeh Lev's battle against "darkness," the evil in the world. The
importance of one's responsibility to others impresses itself upon
the young Asher, and he tries to apply this responsibility to art.
While art is capable of connecting him to others through an understanding of their emotions, that is not its prime function, something which Aryeh Lev understands intuitively.

Jacob Kahn tells Asher that "I talk to God through my sculpture
and painting" (252). He admits, however, that it is not the same
as prayer and later tells Asher, "You will contemplate God and I
will contemplate futility" (260). As Anna Schaeffer tells Asher: "Art
is not for people who want to make the world holy. You will be
like a nun in a bro—in a—theater for burlesque" (209–10). Later,
when Asher is worried about the effect that his crucifixions will
have upon his parents and those members of his community who
come to the exhibition, all Anna Schaeffer can say to him is, "Asher
Lev, you had better pay attention to this matter of taxes and forget
for now about hurting people" (345). For all its ability to provide
Asher with insight into human emotions, art is ultimately presented
as making demands that are very different from the ethical demands
made by Judaism. This disparity between the demands of the two
can be seen most clearly in the artistic and moral issues raised when
Asher must decide whether or not to paint and exhibit his two
Brooklyn Crucifixion paintings.

The problems which Asher faces in relation to his crucifixion
paintings are ones that have been foreshadowed. At the very beginning of the book Asher tells us of the problems these paintings have

caused him; he is still an observant Jew, and "observant Jews do not paint crucifixions" (3). Potok has stated that he "didn't know what kind of crucifixion it was going to be, but I knew I wanted it to be different. I didn't know whether it would be the father or the mother. That, I was willing to let the novel tell me. . . . His father's commitment to his own form of aesthetics—saving people. His mother caught in between."[25]

When Asher begins copying paintings of Jesus in museums, he does so because, as he tells his mother, "I needed the expression, Mama. I couldn't find that expression anywhere else" (172). His father's rage at this does not stop him, his needs as an artist now taking precedence over any parental desires. It is interesting that Potok thinks of the novel as "essentially about a conflict of aesthetics."[26] We have seen his reference to Aryeh Lev's commitment to saving people as a form of aesthetics. This shows the use of the term in a very broad manner: "saving people" being equivalent to an appreciation of the beautiful. Potok sees aesthetics as having the possibility of a moral dimension, particularly the Orthodox Jew's understanding of the term (see note 8). One doubts, however, that Jews such as Aryeh Lev would use the term, if they used it at all, in this way. It is useful to Potok to link these senses of it in this novel as it can be used as a bridge between the two sides of the conflict, a comment of his such as the following becoming comprehensible: "What Asher Lev violates is an unwritten moral aesthetic code, and he violates it because he has no choice; an artist must choose for his art by definition, no matter who's going to be hurt as a result."[27]

The Brooklyn Crucifixion emanates from Asher's guilt feelings toward his mother. In the dust on a bench near Picasso's house in Montmartre, Asher traces his mother's profile—homage given to her who kept his gift alive at great emotional cost. This cost was measured in the pain caused through her being trapped between husband and son—trying to support Aryeh in his needs and beliefs while understanding Asher's uncontrollable need to develop as an artist. Asher's conflict with his father achieves its most tragic form in the anguish of his mother.

The inspiration for the painting comes from Michelangelo's *Pietà*, which in the anguish it depicts becomes one possible model for an expression of all human anguish. After drawing the *Pietà* from memory, Asher is horrified to discover that "the woman supporting the twisted arm of the crucified Jesus bore a faint resemblance to my mother" (314). He destroys this drawing but finds that in another one he leaves out the standing figure of Nicodemus and cannot understand why he did so. Potok implies that this figure has come to represent his father, and by eliminating him Asher may be trying to remove his feelings of guilt at drawing a sculpture so replete with Christian symbolism.

That night his enraged ancestor comes to him in a nightmare, Asher's self criticism tormenting him to the point where he replaces the two Mary figures with bearded males, not unlike his ancestor or father. After this futile attempt to combine the Jewish and Christian traditions, he finds that "The dread was gone. I had no strength left for fighting. I would have to let it lead me now or there would be deeper and deeper layers of the wearying darkness" (317). In these drawings of the *Pietà* and the emotional turmoil they engender, we can see a partial illustration of an oft repeated device which Potok describes as the reader having "to supply from his own being the deliberate gaps which I insert."[28] It is perhaps best described as a method of implication, where silences and actions are not explained and the reader is left to complete the meaning which is implied by the context. In this novel it works well, reader involvement and understanding increasing through being drawn into the process of the completion of meaning; we have seen its flaws in Reuven's silences, more so in *The Promise* than in *The Chosen*.

Eventually, Asher finds that in order to depict his mother's suffering he must use the model of the crucifixion because "there was no aesthetic mold in his own religious tradition into which he could pour a painting of ultimate anguish and torment" (330). He also sees the painting representing all of his own suffering. Potok's depiction of the agony that Asher must suffer in deciding to paint this picture is very well done. Asher's first effort is a good one, but one which does not include a clear crucifix, and he recognizes that it is incomplete. This brings thoughts of his mother's efforts to complete her brother's work, and, indeed, the stress in his family upon completing tasks. He feels he is a fraud and that "it would have made me a whore to leave it incomplete. It would have made it more and more difficult to draw upon that additional aching surge of effort that is always the difference between integrity and deceit in a created work. I would not be a whore to my own existence" (328).

The values fostered in his home by both his mother and father are brought to bear upon the values of the creative artist: honesty, completion of what one has begun, integrity, and the acceptance of the need to push oneself to the limits of one's ability in order to achieve the maximum possible. Thus Asher has taken from his past not so much the values of the Jewish tradition but the ways in which those values have affected his parents' attitudes. He has changed their focus and expression, but in many important ways they still survive.

Despite the fact that after his first attempt to render pain through a crucifixion Asher says that he "felt vaguely unclean, as if I had betrayed a friend" (327), he still believes that there is no other way to do it. One critic thinks that Asher "senses that the crucifixion images and rebellious form are the keys to some truth even more important than tradition."[29] Because the crucifixion has become a symbol often used in Western art to represent the suffering of mankind rather than particularly Christian suffering, it is possible for Asher to use the form of a crucifixion without its religious overtones. Potok explains this in a reference to Picasso, who "at a moment of his life when he was wracked with anguish . . . drew a crucifix. Picasso was by no stretch of the imagination a Christian. Picasso dipped into the forms available to him. He wanted to express his feeling of torment and suffering, and he drew a crucifix."[30]

It may not seem entirely convincing to say that the crucifixion has become so de-Christianized as an artistic form that an artist can use it without the religious overtones remaining strongly present. Potok was questioned closely on this point in an interview he gave at an evangelical college. The interviewer asked him whether in the novel the cross had no religious significance, and how could one have a symbol with no meaning? Potok's reply was that "Art is full of what I call aesthetic vessels, that is to say, motifs which an artist fills with his own being. . . . And since Asher Lev has been studying art from the age of thirteen with the artist/sculptor Kahn, the crucifixion to him was clearly stripped of all its christological salvationist content and was a vessel. To his parents it's what the crucifixion is to most Jews. . . ."[31] It is, of course, the difficulty in grasping, let alone accepting, this concept that ultimately estranges Asher Lev from both his community and parents.

The diction and syntax of the novel are simple and suitable for the creation of an overall sense of restrained tension. There are a number of instances in which strong opinions are expressed in language that is clearly full of emotion but which as in previous novels retains the measured texture of having been filtered through an intellectual sieve rather than coming from the gut. The overall effect is one of evenness and calm but in this novel with strain and unrest underlying it. This style suits these people, who are not violently emotional and not the types to resort to slang or profanity in moments of stress. Because of their inherent decency, they care for the feelings of others, restraining their passions in an attempt to avoid hurting anyone. When strong feelings are expressed, one is aware of forceful attempts at holding wrath in check. In short, the calmness is deceptive, and the style is more complex than appears at first glance.

Not all readers have reacted as positively as this, but comments on the style of this novel have included many more appreciative ones than could be found in relation to Potok's first two novels. While one observer feels that Potok takes Asher too seriously, with the result being an "extremely monotonous solemnity,"[32] another refers to the novel's "finely articulated tragic power" and goes on to say: "Mr. Potok's novels are deceptively plain. He uses no rhetoric, no ostentation of style, neither of which he needs. One feels that his subject was inevitable and that he is writing with deepest and total understanding. . . . His voice is honest and guileless, but most of all it is compassionate. With *My Name Is Asher Lev* Mr. Potok is clearly ending his apprenticeship as a novelist. Each novel has been a step toward mastery. He has written a novel that is little short of a work of genius. . . ."[33]

While one would hesitate to use the term "genius" in describing this novel, it is certainly true that *My Name Is Asher Lev* is a fine piece of work, consistently absorbing, containing tensions vividly rendered, and characters who remain in the mind long after the book is closed because of their struggles to achieve admirable goals while remaining decent human beings. Their inherent decency does not make them weak as characters, and Potok is at least partially correct when he criticizes some of his critics by stating that

Critics of high culture have trouble pigeon-holing my work. One reason is because my books are not in keeping with their central tenets of novel-making, which require an anti-hero, a comic vision, a measure of kinky sex and a good-versus-evil tension. The critics don't know what to make of the world I'm creating. It's a very small esoteric world. The general tendency in modern literature is to polarize. My world is about good people involved in situations that they somehow want to come to terms with in a positive way. Good versus good tends to be regarded by some purveyors of culture as bordering on the Pollyanna-ish.[34]

It is one of Potok's greatest achievements to have shown it possible to create effective novels in which good versus good is the central element. Going against the literary grain of the twentieth century has not been easy, but as he says: "The books have caught on more with people than critics."[35] In novels having the literary quality of these, his comment is not without a certain justifiable accusation.

Chapter Five
In the Beginning
Illness and Accidents

The narrator of Chaim Potok's fourth novel is another highly able child and adolescent, David Lurie. He narrates the story using a method similar to Asher Lev's: he begins as a young man in the present and proceeds to relate in chronological order his boyhood and growing up years. The ending of *In the Beginning* extends somewhat further into the adulthood of the narrator than does that of *My Name Is Asher Lev,* this being necessary for certain plot strands to be tied up.

The narrator relates a childhood of illness and fear, the former caused by an undiagnosed deviated septum, the latter by an extraordinary series of accidents and the presence of bullies. His physical weakness and the fevers caused by his periodic illnesses make him an outsider; his growing academic ability further removes him from the world of boys his age, although he desperately desires to be at one with the world. His father's ties to Europe and the organization that he set up there and which still exists in America extend David's awareness of what constitutes the boundaries of his world. He is initiated into anti-Semitism through his father's memories of it in Europe; the activities of the Am Kedoshim Society and its efforts to help Jews escape from Europe; and the bullying he faces from Eddie Kulanski and his cousin, who have assimilated anti-Semitic attitudes from their European-born parents and express them in America. Being too weak to be able to fight the anti-Semites through the use of physical force, he eventually decides that it must be through words that his battle will be waged.

Against the backdrop of the depression and a rise of anti-Semitism in Europe and America culminating in the concentration camps, David becomes aware of non-Jewish Bible scholars and the way in which they have developed "higher Biblical criticism," which in some instances has become a type of higher anti-Semitism. He becomes determined to fight this by taking a doctorate in biblical studies so that he is equipped to write disputations of their criticisms of the Hebrew Bible. Because he will have to study with non-Jews and Jews who are not observers of the commandments and will be engaged in biblical criticism, he is ostracized by both his fellow yeshiva students and his parents. His new beginning will have to be made on his own.

David Lurie is ill throughout much of the novel, and Potok uses his illness to parallel the state of the world. David tells us that a week after he was born, his mother accidentally tripped, causing him to bang the side of his face and nose on the stone step outside their house. As a result of this fall, he suffers regular bouts of severe illness, which are symbolically extended to events taking place on his block, in America, and in Europe. He also seems particularly accident-prone, the combination of illness and accidents creating a feeling in him of the insecurity and unpredictability of life. There is an implied threat to his religious world view in that the universe seems ruled more by chaos and unsureness than by the dictates of an all-powerful, benevolent deity. At one point David asks, "Why does God make accidents?"[1] His attempt to find an answer to this question will occupy a great deal of his time during the course of the novel, his "Fall" from innocence gaining in prominence as illness and accidents become increasingly central parts of his life.

Max Lurie, David's father, has had his share of "accidents" in his life, and these have had their effect upon David's view of their place in the world. During one of his fevers, David screams in delirium that the death of a canary and a dog, for which he was inadvertently responsible, were accidents. His father says: " 'What isn't an accident?' he asked suddenly in a raging voice. 'When is there ever a time without accidents? . . . Being born a Jew is the biggest accident of all. A man plans and God laughs. God in heaven, if there is a God in this world, how He must laugh! He is not doing his job, Ruth!' " (65–66). Max cannot accept God's presence in a universe apparently ruled by chance. Jews are murdered in wars and pogroms, seemingly powerless to prevent history's "accidents." Evil frequently runs rampant, and God does not prevent it. What is one to make of such a world? Max believes in killing those who try to kill Jews, and he has done this in the Polish army and in an illegal group of Jewish soldiers which he formed to fight anti-Semites in Poland. His physical action does not, however, provide any answers to the problems of good and evil with which his son is so concerned.

In an attempt to escape the world of violence and accidents, David finds solace in bed under the sheet. He says that "This was my quiet world. I had made this world. There were no accidents in this world. I could not understand the world outside. . . . Why did I need my father's world when I had my own world?" (67–68). He dreams of a cleansing flood that will change Eddie Kulanski's and his cousin's hatred to love. This flood will not kill as did the biblical one but change hearts and make the outside world similar to the ideal one he has created beneath his sheets: "when I woke in the morning everything outside would be clean and white and the Angel of Death would have less of a job to do because goyim would not kill Jews and the entire world would be free of accidents. Perhaps the Angel of Death himself would die in the flood; the only one to die" (97–98).

This ideal world proves impossible to bring about, evil being presented as an inherent part of the real world. Potok has stated that "The assertion that historical events of a body of doctrine are somehow linked to an ultimate ontological cause is an expression of the essential nature of the endless human attempt to find unity and meaning in the raw data of experience. Nothing is more typical of the collective Jewish mind, heart, and soul than the preoccupation with this endless search."[2] David attempts to relate both historical events and present day ones to some sort of divine control, to say that at base the universe is under God's tutelage. If God could create a flood to destroy evil in Noah's time, He can create another one to purify the present world. Because of the Jews' particular relationship with God, this, he thinks, should be possible. As one critic puts it: "The young David cannot understand a world replete with violence and accidents, and he attempts to find *meaning* in his personal encounters with violence as well as those experienced by Jews at large."[3] Unfortunately, God does not provide the meaning David seeks, nor does He prevent either the personal or more widespread violence from occurring. After accidentally riding over Eddie Kulanski's hand on his tricycle and bringing forth more hatred, David feels his illness to be almost a relief from a street that "reeked with the odor of malevolence" (149).

The depression, two world wars, and anti-Semitism in Europe and America serve as reference points for evil in the world. Potok frequently presents this evil in terms of accidents, with which history seems replete. Delving into the Jewish tradition, David turns from the safety of his bed to the story of the Golem of Prague, a mythical figure who fought for the Jews when they were threatened. He tries to envisage this legendary figure fighting for Jews in his world, but the forces arrayed against the Golem, particularly the barbarian horde of Nazis, are so great as to make David feel that resistance to the evil "bore increasingly the mark of futility" (270). Eventually the Golem must disappear as a protective force for Jews in David's mind, and he must find some other method of fighting his enemies and, perhaps, discovering whether what he perceives as accidents have any greater significance in explaining evil in the world; is God behind them or are they simply haphazard events in a world without meaning?

Potok has written: "I would prefer to say that the universe is meaningful with pockets of apparent meaninglessness, than to say that it is meaningless with pockets of apparant meaningfulness. In other words, I have questions either way. I see it as my task to attempt to infuse with sense those elements that make no sense. That's the task of man."[4] It is also the task which Potok has given to David Lurie.

Anti-Semitism: Europe and America

In the Beginning is about anti-Semitism, which has directly affected the entire Lurie family. Potok makes it clear that Jew-hatred has a long history and is not dependent upon anything that the Luries in particular have done. There is a continual reference to the European roots of this hatred. Max Lurie, the most extreme example in the novel of the effects of anti-Semitism, shares biographical aspects with Potok's father. Both were followers of the Revisionist Zionist leader Vladimir Jabotinsky, both had their entire families destroyed by the Nazis, and both were soldiers: "He had killed Russians during the First World War as a Polish soldier in the Austrian army. Often I would see him clutching his Yiddish newspaper as he read of the day's events, and I could imagine his veined iron hands holding and firing the machine gun he had used in the war."[5] Max has also killed Russians as a machine gunner and has brought his memories of Europe with him to America. After a series of attacks on Jews in New York City, Max rages: " 'The stinking bastards,' I heard him say as I watched pain and memory crowd themselves into my mother's nervous eyes. 'They brought the poison with them to

America and that German maniac now gives them the courage to spread it. They will destroy America like he is destroying Europe' " (304).

Anti-Semitism is presented as being a European phenomenon that must be transported to the soil of America which would not nourish it on its own. There is some truth in this as American Jews never suffered the endemic Jew-hatred that was directed at them in a number of European countries where anti-Semitism received the support of national governments. Most immigrant groups regardless of their origin or religion suffered some discrimination from those groups more firmly established in the country. In time, this discrimination lessened greatly or died away. Anti-Semitism reached its peak in America in 1935 at the height of the depression, through a combination of economic factors and resistance to large numbers of Jews having made their way up the social and economic ladder. It receded markedly after World War II and has never been a major factor in American-Jewish life with a position comparable in importance to that it held in, say, Poland and Russia.

Potok dramatizes the European source of this hatred through David Lurie's experiences with the Kulanski family. In his recollections of his childhood, David recalls that Eddie Kulanski "hated Jews with the kind of mindless demonic rage that remains incomprehensible—and terrifying—to me to this day. He was only six years old but his hatred bore the breeding of a thousand years" (5). One critic has observed that " 'For Christ's sake,' is the rallying cry employed by Eddie Kulanski and his cousin as they unwittingly echo the Crusaders and their emulators. . . ."[6] He has learned this hatred from his father, and in one of the instances of him persecuting David, his face seems to have "become stony and old. But I know I was imagining it. Hate could not make anyone old" (105).

The stress upon the ancientness, the almost mythological roots of this hatred, heightens the sense of its alienness to the comparatively youthful American context. Indeed, Potok presents through Eddie Kulanski and his cousin the full range of classic anti-Semitic epithets and beliefs. They believe that Jews have horns, suffer from peculiar "Jewish diseases," and have a bad smell. They believe in the accusations against Jews made in the czarist forgery, *The Protocols of the Elders of Zion:* that Jews are working to control the world through their supposed domination of banks and newspapers, that they are Satanic figures. The Kulanskis become the local representatives of the evil that seems in danger of spreading like a cancer from the old to the new world, Potok effectively creating a sense of fear as violence spreads from Eddie and his cousin to anonymous gangs in the neighborhood, to the city itself, to Europe and back again. It seems like a web slowly encompassing the good in society, but Potok makes it clear that good does exist.

While David's father is violently against the "goyim," hardly distinguishing between one gentile and another, even he is shown to recognize that differences exist between non-Jews. His experiences in Europe, including the murder of his brother in a pogrom and a scar on his face from the bayonet of an anti-Semitic Pole, have caused him to detest most gentiles and to express this detestation in strong language. He is particularly appalled by the experience of Tulchin, where the Poles handed over to their Cossack enemies Jews who had fought by their side against the Cossacks, who then murdered the Jews as well as the Poles. When telling David the story, Max omits the fact that there were a number of towns in which the Poles refused to turn over the Jews to their enemies, his hatred of "goyim" making him selective in his historical facts. Yet, Max Lurie can point out that there is no point in expecting gentiles to help Jews fight the Nazis if the Jews do not organize to help themselves, and when the full horror of the concentration camps becomes known, he can say that "The goyim themselves do not understand it" (437). This awareness does not, however, prevent him from carrying a "permanent rage . . . against all the gentile world" (437); he also detests Jews who carry the attitude of Tulchin with them; not being willing to fight for themselves but trusting to gentile good will.

This vacillation in Max's attitude is most effective in depicting the irrational and highly emotional state that the horrors of European anti-Semitism have created in him. Hugh Nissenson has observed that "rarely has the rage of the Jew been so honestly portrayed."[7] It is noteworthy that in his personal dealings with non-Jews in America, this rage is not apparant. Italians are presented as particularly easy for Jews to get along with despite their Catholicism. They do not exhibit any of the anti-Semitism shown by Poles, or Irish policemen who do not rush to stop an attack upon Jews. Mrs. Savanola defends David against Eddie Kulanski, and there is a friendly Italian upstairs in their new apartment house. Max, himself, starts a watch repair business in the shoe shop of an Italian, who praises David's hard work in school.

Italians are not the only Christians who are presented positively. America is seen as markedly different from Europe in its treatment of Jews, even Max being able to praise it:

> "Is America better for Jews, Papa?"
> "Yes."
> "But there are goyim here who hate us."
> "The government does not hate us. That is the difference. The government was made by good Christians. A good Christian is better than an evil high priest" (158)

This is a rather unexpected statement coming from Max, who also feels that coming to America was a wise thing to do because "Here you will not have to kill. We are hated everywhere. But not everyone who hates us kills us. America is not Poland. No place is Poland. Except perhaps Russia" (120). Thus there is a dichotomy presented in attitudes toward non-Jews on the part of even so bitter a character as Max—America *is* different, and, as David's Uncle Meyer tells him, if someone hurts you the courts will punish him: "You don't have to break heads here. . . . This isn't Poland" (161).

One character who was not in Europe during World War I shows most clearly what the effect of America upon Jews can be. Shmuel Bader tells David that he does not hate anyone because no one has ever hurt him. He does not share Max Lurie's experiences and can respond in a balanced way to David's growing hatred of gentiles because of his experiences with the Kulanskis and his father's re-membrances of Europe. Then a new factor, the anti-Semitism of Father Charles Coughlin, preached on the radio and through his magazine, *Social Justice,* enters David's world. The novel is historically sound in its presentation of Coughlin as one of the best-known anti-Semites in America in the 1930s, his diatribes aiding those of American Nazis and the effects of the depression in creating a climate amenable to violence against Jews. Bader gives David a lesson on America. It is a free country, and Coughlin can air his views, but it is not the case that all non-Jews accept what he says: "He is attacked quite frequently by gentiles. . . . They do not all hate us. . . . But there are many good souls among them. They help keep the world alive" (291). While he does not convince David of this, Potok's point is clear: it is as wrong for Jews to lump all gentiles together and consider them evil as it is for gentiles to do this to Jews. Good and bad exist in both groups, and both share a common humanity.

An important link between Europe and America in the novel is the Am Kedoshim Society, founded by Max Lurie just after World War I to fight Polish anti-Semites. Despite having fought with Marshal Pilsudski for Poland, Max and thirty-nine Jewish soldiers found that the Poles still attacked Jews. Their answer to this was to eschew the attitude of Tulchin and fight the Poles. Historically, the period 1917–21 saw a wave of pogroms far worse than the two preceding ones (the 1880s and 1903–6). This third wave was related to revolutions and civil war that occurred in Eastern Europe, and it inspired the creation of many Jewish self-defense groups. The most famous was the Jewish Militia for War against Pogroms, which fought against attacks on Jews in the Ukraine. Potok's presentation of Max Lurie's group thus reflects an actual situation, and his depiction of the death in a pogrom of Max's brother David, who was also Ruth Lurie's first husband, is an important plot device that humanizes the facts of this period. Also, Max's comment that Ruth's parents, still in Poland, would come to America immediately if there was a pogrom and that ritual murder charges against the Jews have cropped up in Lublin and Vilna (in Lithuania), brings the fear experienced during the earlier period in Poland up to the present of the novel's time-scale in America.

The Am Kedoshim Society's continued existence in America reflects the position of Jews in the world. Now a group concerned primarily with getting Jews out of Europe and bringing them to America, where it provides them with financial and other help, Potok presents it as having given up guns for a new type of battle, particularly as the Nazi menace grows. Despite the decency of America, the members of the Society feel that Jews must act for themselves as much as possible. The legacy of European anti-Semitism, the fact of its continued existence, and the spread of it on a smaller though still noticeable scale in America itself has contributed to their awareness of the peculiar position of Jews in the world. As Potok, himself, has said: "Everything that happens in that book is triggered by anti-Semitism."[8] It is his experience of anti-Semitism at the level of his street, and, later, at the much higher level of biblical criticism, that causes David Lurie to decide to fight it as a biblical scholar.

When David expresses an inability to understand "goyim," he is advised to "study Torah and to have nothing to do with them" (124). He develops to a point where he will spend his life studying Torah but with non-Jews as well as Jews. Books, the Hebrew Bible in particular, become increasingly important to him both because he is highly academic and because he sees in them the only way he can carry on the fight in which his father has been engaged throughout his life. In his dreams and imaginings he has used the powerful figure of the Golem to fight the Jews' enemies with violence. However, the Golem proves inadequate to the task, as can be seen when he fails to prevent the Nazis burning books. After this episode, David hugs a volume of Genesis and recovers his speech; he has made the decision to protect as best he can the books that the Jews' enemies have destroyed: he will speak for the books. He has had to go through yet another illness, caused by an accident, which has affected his voice, in order to understand what he really needs: "Books that are true and never change and that you can never stop learning from. . . . I want something firm and fixed, something that won't change every day like the newspapers, something that will make everyone happy that I'm studying it" (275). What he will end up studying, in particular the manner in which he will study the Torah, will not provide him with the "firm and fixed" world he so desires. He will also markedly fail in making everyone happy because of his choice. However, he will succeed in finding a method with which to fight anti-Semitism in his own way.

Religion and Learning

The fearsomeness of the world is partly responsible for David's movement toward scholarship. He sees the Hebrew Bible "as a warm refuge against the hateful, raging world outside" (123), this refuge slowly becoming transformed into the source of conflict between him and the non-Jewish world. Potok has written that

The final confrontation with anti-Semitism comes to this boy from modern Bible criticism. A lot of scholars have used this as a highly sophisticated weapon to get at the Jews. This boy knows that it is a weapon; but he also comes to realize that it contains truths. He asks himself, What do I do? How do I handle the truths. They are being used by Germans. Germans are killing my people. What do I do with those truths? . . . In the end he joins the enemy camp in order to change the face of the enemy. Some of my friends did that. They entered Bible scholarship in order to change the attitude of that discipline toward Jews—and they have succeeded. This is their story.[9]

As in the previous novels, the protagonist is highly talented; he possesses the ability to make use of modern Bible criticism as a weapon against those who would use it against the Jews. Because the major scholars using this new method are German, Potok is able to depict a two fold basis for the resistance to David's intended area of study: it appears to his detractors to question the validity of the Hebrew Bible, and it requires the study of works by people who are not only often anti-Semites but German anti-Semites at that.

This resistance can be seen most clearly in the attitude of Max Lurie, who tells David: " 'I am uncomfortable with German books in my house,' he said after a while 'It is like having a member of an evil family. . . . And I cannot begin to tell you how much I hate the Germans and everything that is German. . . . I will ask you not to read them in my presence' " (374). Max's dislike of David's studying books written by German authors transcends the subject matter of the texts. Even though some of them are written by rabbis, the existence of Hitler makes them unacceptable because of the German language in which they are written.

Max does have other objections shared by many at David's school. He tells David that "German Jewish scholars of the last century had been responsible for the destruction of Torah Judaism" (388). The Jewish enlightenment had its strongest effect in Germany, where Reform Judaism had developed to stop the march to the baptismal font after Jewish emancipation had been achieved. It is arguable whether this had resulted in "the destruction of Torah Judaism." Rather, a reinterpretation of laws and customs occurred based upon scholarly research that was frequently able to point out that what had been considered holy writ was, in reality, merely one possible interpretation of a biblical text by a rabbi or a practice which had become customary but had no particular biblical mandate. In the nineteenth century there had been great resistance to this movement from Orthodox Jewish leaders, just as Potok depicts resistance to scholarly, scientific study of the Bible being greeted by resistance from Orthodoxy in the twentieth century. Although Max tries to accept that David will "fight the goyim with words" (375) while he will use guns, he cannot fully accept David's choice, one which he feels might, however, have been understood by his dead brother, after whom David was named.

David's yeshiva is not a school which insists upon a fundamentalist stance; those are "downtown and in Brooklyn" (390). Nonetheless, his views create resistance on the part of teachers and students, and the library has no books on Bible criticism; he decides not to bring books written in German to school. The reasons for this resistance to scientific biblical criticism go to the roots of Judaism. Potok has stated that "until they confronted major cultures, [Jews] simply never talked about their theological assumptions—or talked about them rarely. Ancient Near Eastern peoples rarely theologized. . . . You see, theology becomes explicit when antagonistic faiths collide or when creed dominates a civilization."[10]

David does not wish to overturn Judaic theology, quite the contrary; he wishes to defend the Torah against those who would dismiss it as irrelevant in the light of Christianity. As he says to his mother in order to justify himself against her remark that he should let others fight those Christian scholars who engage in what one sociology professor at his yeshiva calls the "higher anti-Semitism" (377):

"Which others? Goyim? Or Jews who don't know a thing about Yiddishkeit? It's our Torah they're destroying. Why shouldn't the Jews defend it? Papa fought goyim when they attacked Jews. . . ."

"What I am saying to you is that no one can read such books without being affected by them. In this I agree with your father." (392–93)

David's feeling that he "had entered a war zone, that the battlefield was the Torah, that the casualties were ideas, and that without the danger of serious exposure the field of combat could not be scouted, the nature of the enemy could not be learned . . ." (393) is neither understood nor respected by his family, friends, or those at his yeshiva, with the notable exception of one teacher. In terms of his attempts to convince those most dear to him of the sincerity and validity of his ideas, he is in a similar position to Asher Lev, and Reuven Malter of *The Promise,* both of whom had to fight for their right to believe things other than those held to by the majority of

the members of their communities. At least Reuven had the support
of his father; David, like Asher, is almost completely on his own.

   Potok well understands the importance of Jewish traditions, which
is why the characters within the Jewish community who resist the
protagonist's goals are not presented as stock villains. He has said
that "Tradition is a way of making permanent, of making significant, those things we hold very dear to us and which we think
enhance us as a species."[11] Those characters who wish to preserve
traditional approaches at all cost may not receive the author's admiration, but they certainly do not receive his scorn. He understands
the reasons for their desire to hold firm to traditions for which they,
their families, and their people have suffered and died. In commenting on the need to rethink traditions in the manner in which
David Lurie does, he has observed that "You have to come to an
understanding of how you relate to the tradition without basing
yourself on a fundamentalist version of its sacred text. And that
involves rethinking your relationship to the history of your people.
Many people don't want to do that. . . ."[12] He abjures reliance
upon a fundamentalist approach because his own studies have shown
him that this approach cannot be justified by the facts. Also, fundamentalism does not permit the use of ideas from outside the Jewish
tradition, even when those ideas might add a great deal to the
tradition. Of course a fundamentalist like Reb Saunders or Rav
Kalman would be unlikely to perceive anything of value in a non-
Jewish culture, and it is this narrowness of vision which Potok
resists.

   David Lurie's reading does lead him to certain conclusions even
while still a yeshiva student that would cause those who are suspicious of his studies to feel that he had been adversely affected by
them. Despite his love of the Torah, he comes to believe that "The
Torah is not the word of God to Moses at Sinai. But neither is it
infantile stores and fables and legends and borrowed pagan
myths. . . . I have to go to the secular world for new tools to find
out what it is. My Orthodox world detests and is terrified by those
tools. . . . I want to know the truth about the beginnings of my
people" (437). His belief that the Torah does not consist of divine
revelation to Moses would make him anathema to his Jewish community. His proviso that it is more than stories, fables, legends,

and myths would not have sufficient weight to exonerate him from
charges of apostasy in an Orthodox environment.

Potok touched upon this problem a decade earlier in a review of
Rabbi Louis Jacobs' book, *the Principles of Jewish Faith*. In his review
Potok stated that Rabbi Jacobs

does not recognize the great extent to which the whole fabric of Jewish
doctrine is held together by the thread of fundamentalist revelation. Rabbi
Jacobs is correct in removing that thread, but he will not admit that he
thereby begins to unravel the entire fabric. . . .

Indeed, it is because the entire fabric of belief is imperiled that those
who are still deeply committed to Judaism, and at the same time are aware
of the radical challenge of modernism, undergo the difficulties of rethinking their positions. . . .

Along with its scholarly discussion of classical Jewish theology, the
value of his book comes from its honest groping for an alternative to
fundamentalism. . . . Thus the most refreshing element in the book is
Rabbi Jacobs's recognition of the validity of modern biblical criticism,
though this has been taken for granted by Jewish theologians in America
for many years now. [13]

Although Potok does not feel that Louis Jacobs satisfactorily
discusses in this book the problems of fundamentalism versus the
new problems facing Judaism, he admires his attempts to grapple
with these difficulties. Similarly, David Lurie recognizes the existence of the challenge of modernist thought but does not come to
grips with the problem of the unraveling of "the entire fabric" which
an attack on fundamentalism can cause. But, then, David Lurie is
at the beginning of his career, the focus of the novel being not upon
his solutions to the conflict between fundamentalism and modern
biblical criticism but his awareness that this criticism cannot be
ignored and must be faced. He is also aware that the modern scientific method can be used to throw new and valuable light on the
origins of the Hebrew Bible, his desire being both to fight the
negative use of this method by certain scholars and to show the
positive value it can have in explaining the sources of the Torah.
The implication at the end of the novel is that he retains his sense
of the value of the past while proceeding to nourish the present
(453).

The critical method at the root of David's problems involves
textual emendation of words that do not fit the meaning of a par-

ticular passage, and the recognition of emendations by earlier commentators to explain unclear passages. When in his biblical studies at the yeshiva David questions the meaning of certain verses, he is surprised to find that Rashi, the greatest of all the medieval Jewish commentators on the Bible and Talmud, has seen fit to transpose verses and has explained others by making deductions that do not appear directly in the text. There is even the hint in some commentators that certain passages in the Torah could date from post-Mosaic times, a heretical attitude if one is to believe that all of the Torah was revealed to Moses at Sinai. The only support David receives in his interest in these matters comes from a somewhat unexpected source: Rav Tuvya Sharfman, who is described as "the greatest Talmudist in the Orthodox Jewish world . . ." (404). During one of his Talmud classes, David presents an explanation of a difficult passage by citing the Meiri, a great early medieval Talmud commentator. Rav Sharfman shouts at him that "if the Meiri was in my class and said that, I would throw him out" (410). He then proceeds to offer a brilliant explanation of his own. Sharfman's willingness to question some of the views of the traditionally accepted commentators explains his interest in David's outside reading of biblical critics with his only criticism being that they tend to be shallow; he is not against their methods and does not mind that most are not Jewish and are secularists.

Rav Sharfman differs from Potok's other rabbis in that he is a Lithuanian, not Polish or Russian. The Lithuanian Jews had a reputation for rationality and intellectuality greatly at variance with that of the Hasidim, whose emotional approach to Jewish texts seemed to the Lithuanians to avoid reason and border on superstition. In addition to being from Lithuania, where he was ordained by his grandfather, Sharfman holds a doctorate in philosophy from the University of Berlin. The German connection aids in understanding his more modern approach to Bible and Talmudic studies and, interestingly, relates him to those Bible scholars of German origin about whom David is so interested and the reading of whose books have created such difficulties for him at home and at school.

Rav Sharfman gives David the support he needs to continue his studies in an unorthodox direction while remaining tied to his Jewish heritage. He does not believe that the commentators have said the final word. Given the mass murder of Europe's Jews, it is to him of the greatest importance that the survivors try to create "living

waters of our own" (421). He recognizes the price that David will
have to pay, the suspicion he will arouse in both Jew and gentile
because of their fear that he is questioning ideas they hold sacred.
However, since David is rooted in the Jewish world, Sharfman
believes that he is best equipped to do this work, to see what value
the Bible holds today.

In his own work on the translation of the Hebrew Bible, Potok
states that the team of scholars was "working with elements from
the cores of two great civilizations—the Bible on the one hand, and
a radical, new and in many ways, quite heartless scholarly meth-
odology on the other, the techniques of scientific biblical criticism.
We were attempting to create a work that would speak to two
civilizations—Judaism and secular humanism—simultaneously."[14]
In his attribution of "heartlessness" to scientific biblical criticism,
Potok recognizes the emotional involvement that he as well as others
have in the Hebrew Bible; it is not just any book. David Lurie also
recognizes this involvement in others because he possesses it himself.
Unlike Potok in his translation, David Lurie is not particularly
concerned with making his work "speak" to secular humanism. He
is concerned with a defense of the Torah against its detractors, be
they secular humanists, Christians, or Jews. In using the tools of
secular humanism he will cause pain, but his goal is not that; it is
his love of the Torah that makes him want to defend it.

Through his brother Alex, Potok illustrates David's integrity.
Alex's opinion of the Hebrew Bible startles David:

"If you keep quiet, no one knows what you think. Why do you have
to study it and publish books about it and make a fuss and get everyone
upset?"

I stared at him.

"God, Davey, I read Darwin a while ago and it's all a bunch of Sunday
school stories. I get more out of a good novel." (438)

David realizes that his brother is simply going through the motions
of religious observance for his parents' sake; he will probably cease
his observance of the commandments as soon as he leaves home.
This contrast between the attitudes of the two brothers works well.
David Lurie is similar in some respects to his dead uncle David
who, as his father tells him, "used to tell me he was searching for
truth. He did not care what precious ideas he threw aside once he

thought them untrue. I did not like that about my brother David. He was gentle in everything except the use of his mind" (444). What Max does not realize is the strong love his son has for the Torah and how much he does care for the "precious ideas" that his father thinks he would be so willing to cast aside.

Style

In the Beginning contains some marked stylistic developments in comparison to Potok's earlier novels. The primary ones lie in Potok's use of flashbacks and impressionistic techniques, which are most effective in conveying the state of David's mind during feelings of tension, fear, or when fever afflicts him. In *My Name Is Asher Lev* and *In the Beginning* Potok uses extended flashbacks, the protagonists relating events that occurred before the point when the novel begins. However, the movement to the past and back again to the present occurring a number of times during the course of a narrative creates problems of integration that are not faced when a novel contains only an initial flashback and remains in the narrator's memory throughout. *In the Beginning* contains a much more complex use of the flashback technique than does *My Name Is Asher Lev*. In one example, one finds that David's cousin Saul has accidentally fallen and cut his lip. The sight of the swollen lip serves as a jumping off point for David's remembrances of one of his periods of illness. His recollections contain references to his obsession with accidents but place much stress upon his father and mother and the problems they face in getting his mother's parents to leave Poland. Through David's recall of their conversation, Potok informs us of Max's attitude toward the nature of the Jews' place in the world (Jews are more prone than others to suffer from the "accidents" of history) and of David's wish to have the biblical giant Og chastise Eddie Kulanski and his cousin and so create a peaceful world away from the horrors of the real one. The interesting aspect of this daydream is the variety of concerns it contains: current events, history, biblical references, and David's own fears. The motif of sleep, Saul's and David's, is used for a skillful entry into the past and return to the present.

A more risky flashback combines David's fears with his father's past. A first-person narrator cannot know things that he has not seen, overheard, read, or been told. However, Potok succeeds in presenting a vivid sense of what Max's experience of fighting Poles

and Cossacks *might* have been like. Because of his continual immersion in stories of his father's fighting past in Europe and the
role played by the Am Kedoshim Society, David experiences a hal-
lucination that transforms an American forest into an East European
battleground. He imagines what his father did, peopling the woods
with armed Am Kedoshim Society members and imagining the
existence of their enemies near at hand. He imagines the wedding
of his Uncle David and his mother in the woods, guarded against
those who would make pogroms. Potok uses a boy's playing at
soldier to depict Max Lurie's past as well as his son's understanding
of it. David's play takes on an importance beyond mere play: it
becomes his way of assimilating what he has heard of his father's
experiences and of helping him to fight actively against the perse-
cutors of Jews. His father's physical strength and courage can, through
his imagination, bolster his own helplessness. It is noteworthy that
at one point David imagines himself shooting dead with his branch-
machine gun Eddie Kulanski and his cousin. The reenactment of
his father's past provides him with strength to destroy his present
enemies. This imaginary strength helps him in a realistic way, as
he states that "I realized with astonishment that I had not been ill
during all the weeks we had been away and that I had had only one
minor accident" (175). The combination of removal from the terror
of his street and an imagined ability to deal with his tormentors
appears to have made him healthier.

Potok's use of impressionistic imagery can be seen in his descriptions of a braided Havdalah candle, whose "tip danced and spiraled
and reached out into the enshrouding darkness . . ." (16). This is
a favorite image of Potok's to describe his attitude toward the world;
he has written: "I would rather try to discover some light in the
patches of darkness than extend the darkness to wherever there is
now light."[15] The light of the candle reaching out into the darkness,
and its demise when "The flame sputtered, fought for life, and died.
There was a moment of total darkness" (17) symbolize for Potok
the fragility of "light" in the world and the necessity of fostering
its existence wherever possible.

David's mother and father leave his dark bedroom at night and
walk into the light of the hall. He sees himself as a "dark" force,
his parents glad to be with each other in the light. They are, he
thinks, relieved to be away from his persistent illness, and his bouts

of fever are described in highly visual imagery with light and colors predominating—hallucinatory, nightmarish effects being created.

In terms of diction, this is the first novel in which Potok creates characters who use profanity. Thus, Max Lurie frequently breaks into rages and refers to people as "bastards," and Eddie Kulanski's hatred of Jews is realistically expressed when he shouts at David, "You fucking kike. My father says you stink up the world" (104). Because anti-Semitism is central to this novel, the tone is much more harsh than in the previous novels, although one has a hint of this tone in *My Name Is Asher Lev* in Aryeh Lev's responses to the news of the persecution of Jews in Russia. As one reviewer put it: "The book has an ascetic, stoical, almost self-punishing tone, established with its first line, 'All beginnings are hard' . . . a heavy earnestness pervades it all."[16]

This earnestness can become oppressive, with the problems of the world further compounded by the protagonist's chronic illness and a feeling that both he and the Jewishness for which he is fighting are depressingly uninspiring. There is no joy to be seen in either the protagonist or a Judaism under seige, when surely the survival of Judaism has at least partially been due to the joy that it inspired in its adherents as well as to the sense of duty and responsibility that it engendered. The bleakness of the personality of the protagonist tends to carry over to his main interest—Judaism. While David Lurie undoubtedly loves his religion and wishes to devote his life to its defense, one could have done with a bit of spontaneous joy in its practice. Perhaps this is too much to expect given the times and subject that are the concerns of this novel, but Potok has a tendency to view Judaism primarily through academic lenses. When this is combined with a character who lacks the interest and appeal of a Danny Saunders, Reuven Malter, or Asher Lev the heaviness of the narrative can cast a gloom over areas which, one expects, Potok does not wish the reader to see in this overcast light.

Some lightness occurs in a rather good touch: Rav Sharfman's use of baseball terminology during Talmudic discussions. Although he is present in the novel for only a brief period, Sharfman is one of the more effective characters, much more so than Mr. Samuel Bader, who remains stiff and distant. The speech patterns of Max Lurie are also rendered effectively through a use of slang and forceful phraseology. A statement that at home only Yiddish is spoken and neither Max nor Ruth speak English well is necessary since we would not know this from the dialogue; however, the fact that Potok must make such a comment is a weakness.

The structure of the novel is based upon the book of Genesis which, of course, begins with the words, "In the beginning. . . ." There is a stress upon the importance of creation, with David Lurie slowly reaching a point where he is committed to a revitalization of Jewish thought, an effort wherein the six chapters of the novel describing his progress parallel the six days of creation. His illness and recovery repeated many times; his position as an outsider because of his weakness and intelligence; and his intellectual development over time provide parallels with the state of the Jewish people.

A broader relationship between the historical events described in the novel and the Genesis chapter can be seen in Lillian Kremer's observation that "Potok's portrayal of Judaism emerging from the Holocaust to rebirth in America and Israel parallels the conclusion of Genesis when Joseph recapitulates the lesson of his career, teaching that God brings good out of evil; that he will deliver the Jewish people out of Egypt and bring them to the land He promised the patriarchs."[17]

In this novel, as in the previous ones, Potok is able to integrate history into the plot so that it plays an active part in the characterizations. *In the Beginning* shows an advance in his ability to structure a novel, to write convincing dialogue, and to use impressionistic and stream-of-consciousness techniques to present various strands of thought as they affect a character. The tale is fascinating, if frequently overly oppressive. It does show that Potok has become extremely adept at creating the form of novel known as the bildungsroman. Perhaps he is now due for a move into a different form where an adult is the protagonist. Potok has shown that he need not restrict himself to youths, for Max Lurie is the most successful character in this novel. *In the Beginning,* even with its faults, is impressive and shows Potok's steadily increasing skill as a novelist.

Chapter Six
Wanderings: Chaim Potok's History of the Jews

Wanderings is Potok's longest work of nonfiction, his others being a compilation of pamphlets, and essays. Potok saw the book as both worthwhile as an end in itself and as having certain subsidiary benefits to his work as a novelist. In an interview he said that

"It was really an effort to see how I related to the culture package called Judaism, and its beginnings. I needed it to clear the deck for the next novel *(The Book of Lights)*, because that was going to be a confrontation with Asiatic Paganism. I wanted to know what was being confronted. . . ."

The initial idea for *Wanderings* came from Potok's editor at the Alfred Knopf Co. "He thought it might be interesting to have a book on Judaism that everybody would like to read."

The project turned into much more for Potok. "*Wanderings* made clear to me what that culture package (Judaism) was. I wanted to know what it borrowed, and what it gave back to the world."[1]

Wanderings may be seen as Potok's attempt to bring together his ideas concerning Judaism in a form that would demand a level of scholarly rigor greater than had been required by his novels. This rigor would provide a different lense through which to view the cultural confrontations with which Judaism has been concerned throughout its history. This approach was to be balanced by the requirement to create a story of Judaism that would have a popular appeal, a book that "everybody would like to read." A combination of the scholarly and the popular would appear to create an impossible union; however, Potok has managed much better than could have been expected in reconciling the demands of these two disparate qualities. Inevitably, something has been lost from each aspect: the scholarship having to give way at times to a somewhat unhistorical approach; the accessibility of the narrative lessening for a mass audience as the demands of scholarship necessitated a careful scrutiny of historical minutiae.

Potok's approach is to show what the various civilizations in which the Jews have lived and those which have affected them by their proximity have contributed to Judaism and Jewish culture. He is also concerned to show what the Jews contributed to these other cultures. His view of the Hebrew Bible is not a fundamentalist one, and he shows no difficulty in granting to pagan and other non-Jewish cultures attributes that a more fundamentalist rabbi would not be likely to grant. He points out, for example, that the war with the Canaanites went on for two hundred years, but that there was also "a seven-hundred-year-long culture war, which the Israelites came close to losing many times. The Bible makes no attempt to offer us an objective picture of Canaanite civilization."[2]

At least part of his reason for holding this viewpoint may lie in his reading of the Jewish scholar Yehezkel Kaufmann. In a review of Kaufmann's work in an obituary, Potok states Kaufmann's belief that "the Bible is not at all a polemic against paganism, that it cannot be regarded as such because it does not begin to understand the real nature of paganism; . . . the Bible appears always to be under the impression that pagans worshipped gods of wood and stone, which is certainly not what the pagans themselves believed. . . . The pagan gods were personified symbols of these forces of nature and were themselves subject to this supernatural power. It was this power which was the true object of pagan worship."[3] If it is the power *behind* the sun, moon, earth, and sea that paganism worships, the distance from it to Jehovah, although still very great, is not quite as great as may have been thought.

Potok points out that while Judaism can claim to have developed monotheism to its highest degree, the Egyptian pharaoh Akhenaten developed the worship of Aten, the god that is represented by the sun: "Atenism made no ethical demands upon the worshipper other than loving gratitude. It was a deeply felt worship of one aspect of nature: the sun. Scholarly debate about the precise nature of Atenism—was it a pure or rudimentary monotheism?—still goes on. It appears to have possessed a striking feature of later monotheism: intolerance. Akhenaten sent workmen throughout the land to obliterate with hammer and chisel the names of the many gods of Egypt" (58).

Pure monotheism came slowly to the Israelites, as Potok states that during the first two centuries in Canaan they frequently worshipped the local pagan deities. He sees this in a matter of fact way, reflecting his down to earth attitude toward the development of his people: "When you descend from your wandering donkey and become tied to a plot of ground upon whose fertility your life depends, you might not hesitate to invoke a pagan god or goddess as added security against the dread of famine" (92). The effects of the experience at Sinai needed time to take hold, and it is an admirable part of this history that Potok does not become an apologist for or attempt to gloss over facts and opinions that might well not be particularly popular with the Jewish readership of the book. It is noteworthy that in his review of Yehezkel Kaufmann's ideas, Potok writes that "Kaufmann never denied that Israel borrowed many of its forms of worship from pagan nations, but he claimed that what it borrowed it completely transformed and absorbed into its zealous monotheism."[4] However, the transformation inspired by Sinai would take time.

Potok presents the events at Sinai with a mixture of reverence and rational analysis. After pointing out that the description of the event in the Hebrew Bible shows the difficulty the author(s) had in expressing its significance through words, Potok presents the possible ways of viewing it. It is presented as a supernatural event, but do we view Moses "as the intermediary between YHWH and the people, or as the divinely inspired author—the difference between the two views is vast, and we must each of us decide how we see this event . . ." (76). However we interpret Moses' role here, he remains in contact with the Divine. Potok, however, presents the questions that have arisen concerning the origin of the Ten Commandments; questions, that is, that have arisen to nonfundamentalist scholars: "We do not know if the Decalogue that has come down to us in the text of Exodus was actually the one transmitted by Moses or was given final form in a later time. It differs in some respects from the Decalogue in Deuteronomy 5:2–18. Both Decalogues may have had their origins in a third, older, briefer version suggested by scholars . . ." (78). He goes on to point out that later rabbis moved passages about in order to attempt a reconciliation of the various parts.

The covenant between YHWH and the Hebrew people was in the form of a suzerainty treaty, a type of agreement common at the time. Potok asks whether the content of this treaty, "most particularly its first sections, was directly the creation of—YHWH? Moses? The people? All three, at Sinai? All three during the desert wandering? Later history? All the traditions available to the writer connected that covenant to Sinai, and that was the way he wrote it, giving them all equal validity. What right had he to choose among them which was true and which was not?" (79).

That Potok, a rabbi, asks these questions in a popular history is to his credit. His respect for individual interpretation based upon an awareness of the known facts is high, the possibility of a number of interpretations not affecting the underlying spiritual importance of the issues in question. Thus, despite the questions he raises, he can state that the experience of the Jewish people at Mount Sinai constitutes a new vision of man's relationship to the universe that cannot be seen in terms of a slow growth out of previous ideas: "It is an epiphany, an inductive leap of extraordinary seminality, or a vaulting of the imagination—call it what you wish. The people at the foot of that mountain, as well as millennia of their offspring, believed that the covenant had been given to them by YHWH" (76). That leap of the imagination, Potok shows, has changed the course of human history however one interprets the details of what actually happened. Another slant on Potok's view of Sinai may be seen in his remark that "I *do* believe that it isn't a blind swirl of forces. I cannot see history in that fashion at all. It is meaningful to me in the sense that it is a record of my species and I can look at it and learn from it. . . . I think that to a very great extent we are partners with the divine in this enterprise called history."[5] Thus, history has a meaning in which man and God play their part and in which one can perceive man's attempts to make sense of his world.

The fact that the author is a novelist can be seen in a number of instances, not least of which is his tendency to focus upon individuals as exemplars of particular cultural or historical periods. Despite the overall structure of the book as a series of culture confrontations between Judaism and a number of other cultures, the role of individuals in Jewish and non-Jewish history is presented as vital. Indeed, Potok has said:

But the book is about people, not cultural dynamics. I walked through all of these cultures through the books I read, and I tried to translate abstract scholarship into people.

This is why *Wanderings* is laced with numerous portraits of breathing historical figures, each seen in social and cultural contexts, figures such as Moses, Ezekiel, Saul, Jesus Christ. I was fascinated to discover how the direction of our species changed at different times because of a single person. . . . This is almost a pattern of our species, the power of the individual dream."[6]

Potok's treatment of historical figures frequently gives them the feel of characters in a novel but with historical fact to bolster the characterizations. In his presentation of Moses, for example, he tries to understand how Moses' mind might have responded to situations in which he found himself. He even requests that we grant him a certain amount of poetic licence: "Perhaps I can be permitted the freedom of the novelist at this point. Moses lived for decades among the Midianites. There is no way we can penetrate the turns of his mind during that time except through an act of the imagination. With an awareness of doing violence to reality but with the hope of performing some service to clarity, I present this simplified and schematic account of his thoughts, straightening the curves and convolutions and making of decades of lost trails and new paths a single straight road" (66). Potok then proceeds to try to explain how Moses' relationship with YHWH developed to a point where he became the leader of a slave people and led them out of Egypt. It is history with the addition of inference, somewhat similar to what Bernard Malamud does in *The Fixer,* where he relates what his novelist's insight tells him might have been the unrecorded thought processes of Yakov Bok (Mendel Beilis).

Potok does not attempt an explanation of the thought processes of all the many historical figures upon whom he focuses, but in each instance shows how they relate to their time, reflecting and diverging from it. The effect is a humanization of the historical events, Potok furthering this by personalizing the descriptions of certain of these figures. About Rashi, the medieval Talmudic commentator, he writes: "He entered my life when I was a child and has remained a permanent resident in the Jewish civilization I carry within myself" (301). Potok further personalizes his reference to Rashi by presenting him as a concerned teacher: "He seems in the room with you, anticipating the problems you will have with the text, waiting for your questions, then answering them briefly, simply, with a clear aversion for convoluted thought" (302). Rashi moves from being solely an eleventh-century master Talmudist to being an individual whose influence continues to be strongly felt

in the Jewish world of the twentieth century. Indeed, Potok says
that "I do not know if the Talmud would be at all accessible today
were it not for the commentary of Rashi" (302). Thus, Rashi's
attempts to aid medieval Jews' understanding of Talmudic and
biblical texts have been of direct help to the author of *Wanderings,*
and he is therefore seen as more than a historical figure.

The twelfth-century scholar Maimonides reflects views seen in
many of Potok's novels. As we have seen, Potok is primarily concerned with issues involved in cultural confrontation between Judaism and other cultures; he presents Maimonides as also involved
in this area. Like Potok's characters in his novels, Maimonides faced
great difficulties with Orthodox Jewish authorities when he diverged
from accepted practice by attempting to show the relevance of Greek
and rational thought to Judaism. Potok describes the root of Maimonides's problem as follows:

These are the two essentially irreconcilable elements at the very core of
Judaism, the one rational, facing outward toward the world and general
culture, eager for all worthwhile knowledge, prepared to enter the mar-
ketplace of ideas; the other mystical, facing inward toward its own sources,
possessed of its unalloyed vision of Jewish destiny, feeding off its inner
strength and rejecting vehemently and with no small measure of contempt
any distortion of its vision of reality from civilizations alien to what it
sees as the pure essence of Judaism. These two elements at the core of the
Jewish tradition, rubbing up against each other, generate the friction and
bitterness of controversy and, one hopes, the sparks of creativity. (314)

Just as Potok's protagonists suffered resistance, ostracism, and
veritable persecution for their views, so Maimonides was persecuted
by the Jewish authorities to the extent of his books being burned
by the Inquisition who, Potok states, were probably informed of
his heretical ideas by Jews antagonistic to his views. One cannot
but feel Potok's sympathy for him and see reflected in the tribulations of Danny Saunders, Reuven Malter, Asher Lev, David Lurie,
and Davita Chandal the problems encountered with a rigid Orthodoxy when individuals reach out to a wider world for new or different
knowledge and ideas. In addition, the tone and content of the above
quotation states Potok's views of problems that are, in his opinion,
"at the very core of Judaism" so that he is clearly making a statement
that applies to more than Maimonides's problems alone: it applies
to Potok's major concerns as a novelist, which emanate from his

interpretation of Jewish history. His interpretation of history and his concerns as a novelist feed each other, and in reading his historical interpretations as set out in *Wanderings* one can gain insights into Potok as a novelist.

Wanderings frequently has the feel of a novel despite Potok's solid scholarship. One critic comments that "Potok introduces no new philosophical or social concepts, nor does he look at history with an anthropologist's or sociologist's eyes. This is history as narrative, a novelist's personal, tour-guided journey through time and space, among a people with whom the author is genuinely and affectionately involved. . . . The personal touch is everywhere. . . ."[7] The "personal touch" takes the form of comment upon, and disagreement with, a fundamentalist biblical stance; queries relating to what the people may have felt during a particular event; references to the literary style of portions of the Bible presented through a novelist's eye; and a frequent use of imagery and startling contrasts and facts.

Just as Potok tries to understand how a central figure like Moses may have perceived the tumultuous events through which he passed and was partially instrumental in causing, so he wonders how a particular Hebrew might have understood events affecting him. Solomon's temple in Jerusalem shared certain forms with the Canaanite paganism which it stood against. Thus, "the sacred ark was placed, and the presence of YHWH resided enthroned upon two huge, human-headed, lion-bodied, winged creatures called cherubim" (114). Potok writes of the probable bewilderment of the Israelite coming to Jerusalem to see this "house of YHWH." This puzzlement could have been caused by an inability to separate the new monotheistic religion from that of the pagans who surrounded him. Potok remarks that "there is no way we can understand what an Israelite of that time thought he saw . . ." as he gazed at the temple architecture and decorations: "When he looked at the tall freestanding pillars, did he envisage matzevot, the standing stones— fertility symbols, perhaps—of Canaanite paganism, or did he see only beautifully designed pillars? We have no way of knowing" (114).

Potok does not try to enter the mind of this average Israelite because it is impossible to do so. Unlike the situation with Moses, there is no information upon which he can base a judgment. However, the question he raises is not without value. History which dwells solely upon grand intellectual and political movements while ignoring even a mention of their effects upon the individual leaves a great deal unconsidered. What Potok achieves by raising the question of the effects on an individual living in a time when he is under the pressure of transition between two different religious world views is a feeling of empathy on the part of the reader with his imaginary Israelite: a bringing down to earth of the effects of the new vision on the unsophisticated mind. One critic has observed that "Mr. Potok has centered everything on producing a narrative of dramatic immediacy, including evocations of the landscapes through which the Jews passed and the psychological dimensions of their ordeals. In short, this is the story of Jewish history *told* as a story. How successful is Mr. Potok in this venture? As history, *Wanderings* is responsible, comprehensive and in touch with 20th century research. These are qualities that could have been lost in the rush to tell a good story but were not."[8]

Potok is interested in the literary style of the Hebrew Bible, the form as well as the content. Referring to the style of the covenant treaty between Jehovah and the Hebrews, Potok states that the writer "offered us not a straight narrative but a prismatic, almost surrealistic one filled with splintered, uneven, broken sequences, repetitions, elisions, contradictions, attempting with words to trap the elusive heart of the event to convey somehow its infinitely mysterious dimensions—and probably failing, as I am failing now in my attempt to describe his effort" (79). His stress here is upon the difficulty if not the impossibility of words to describe the mystery of the contact made between God and man. His admiration for the struggle made by the biblical writer comes through nonetheless; it is this struggle that is important, for it shows the writer's commitment to an attempt to understand and relate the ineffable.

In discussing one of the five probable authors of the Hebrew Bible, Potok notes the wide range of sources which this author used. The *J* author, so called because he used the name YHWH, Jehovah, for God, brought together numerous strands to create a unified narrative. Potok states that "He or she" was a writer of "incalculable genius, gifted beyond measure with a purity of narrative style and a sharply focussed vision of the moral interplay between YHWH and man" (117). To give his vision expression, "he used every available literary form at his disposal, gathered from all the world of the ancient Near East. At times he consciously repeated lines from ancient myths, replacing the nature-rooted, cult-demanding, and often whimsical callousness of the gods with the moral and ethical imperative of YHWH; at other times he utilized the outlines of old tales and filled them with Israelite content. Often, as in the account of the sacrifice of Isaac, no prototype is known to us and we are presented with what appears to be an original narrative . . ." (117). The manner in which Potok presents these facts shows that he finds no difficulty in considering aspects of the Hebrew Bible from a purely literary vantage point. Of course, this does not negate the spiritual value of the ideas expressed; however, it does show Potok's multiple orientation in *Wanderings:* the historian, the novelist, and, to a lesser extent, the rabbi.

Potok has written of his underlying religious reading of the Bible: "Beyond it all, and at the same time deep within it, reaching down to the very lowest levels of existence, was a presence—the only real hero, as it were, in the Hebrew Bible . . . a passionate and caring presence, a Being who was like a father with a child he deeply loves and to whom all those struggling humans were reaching out."[9] This presence is clearest in the Hebrew Bible; after the biblical period the concern of the Jews with this presence still underlies the historical events which Potok relates, and his commitment to it, as with that of the Jewish people, permeates *Wanderings.* Indeed, one critic has written that "The narrative is woven with a religious motif. Potok's God is not some abstract deity in a history book—it is his God. The Bible is not a collection of ancient tales—but the true Book of his people. The Jews are not some anthropological group—but his own flesh and blood."[10]

Potok sees religious sages supporting his view of the acceptability of interpretation of Jewish law to meet changing circumstances. He cites the views of Hillel, who believed "it necessary to expand the law and apply it with fresh vision to each new generation. . . . [Hillel believed in searching for] new methods of deriving meaning from the sacred texts that would enable the law to be applied to unforeseen realities" (224). Rabbi Judah the Prince, who began the work of editing the Mishnah, "altered the original language when it obscured a matter of law (he and his court would decide upon the proper law and that would be made the language of the text) . . . ." (229). This is close to the position held by David and Reuven Malter and David Lurie. While they would not "decide upon the proper law" they did feel it acceptable to emmend a text when evidence justified so doing. One sees, therefore, attitudes that first make their appearance in the novels brought forth in a historical context in *Wanderings*—fiction and nonfiction supporting each other.

Potok's style in *Wanderings* frequently diverges from that of the strict historian through his use of imagery and stark contrasts. These achieve literary effects that heighten the sense of the historical issues being presented. He also includes some rather outlandish facts that provide comic relief as well as an insight into a particular facet of historical experience. One can see his use of imagery in a description of Islam: "The high god of the Bedouin was the moon, by whose silver-white light he grazed his flocks and whose benevolence cooled the air and moistened the ground. Once I saw a full moon rise over Arabia on a chill April night; no, it seemed to leap from its underground cavern. The strange magic of optical illusion gave it a sky-filling vastness, and I could sense how it might be worshipped as a god, this life-giving lamp that replaced the killing sun of the day" (249). The use of multiple images here which appeal to the senses of feel and sight, and the personification of the moon, enrich the merely factual statement of the basis of the Bedouin's reasons for moon worship. The rhetorical device of disagreeing with his own observation before stating a final judgment takes the reader into the thought process involved in the experience giving a conversational, oral, feel to the description.

Potok frequently uses surprising contrasts to highlight the importance of an event or situation. For instance, the first sentence of the final section of the book is set off on its own; it reads, "On May 31, 1665, the Messiah came" (335). Then follows two and a half pages of explanation of the situation of the Jews at this particular time. It is not until three pages after the sentence appears that the name Sabbatai Zevi occurs and his story is told. Since the book is intended to have a wide audience and popular appeal, it is probable that large numbers of people will not even have heard of this man and the suspense factor will be considerable. The element of contrast comes into play in the positioning of the line at the beginning of a section that is immediately preceeded by discussion of the trials of the ghetto period and the exile. In its starkness, the line has a shock value that attempts to parallel what the effect of the news must have been upon the Jews of the time.

There are numerous instances of Potok's use of contrasting ideas. His description of the site in Madrid of an auto-da-fé in the seventeenth century as it now is—"There are pigeons and children.

An old man was selling toys" (325)—heightens one's sense of the horrors of the earlier event. In his description of the attributes of modern paganism or secular humanism, he tells us that "it is probably the most creative, the most liberated, the wealthiest, most dehumanizing, and most murderous civilization in the history of our species" (359). The first three attributes in no way prepare us for the last two; but Jews have suffered terribly as a result of secularism, and Potok shocks us into a reminder of that fact.

The frequent weightiness of this history is lightened by comic relief. Thus, the atrocities of the Chmielnicki period are described as "a bloody peasant war, and Jews were simply caught in the middle. Perhaps they wondered how you sanctified the Name of God when you died at the hands of a mounted sword-wielding cossack because you were a tax farmer for a Polish squire" (348). One does not laugh aloud at such a comment, but the absurdity of these massacres is highlighted.

We learn that "A Bedouin brought to a halt by a violent sandstorm or caught up in some emergency can thrust a branch down the throat of a camel and find its regurgitated water drinkable if it is not older than a day or two. There are about a thousand names for the camel in Arabic, almost as many synonyms as are used for the sword" (248). We are also informed that part of the reason for the increase in population from the end of the eighteenth century to the beginning of World War I was "the introduction of cotton undergarments, which could be laundered in boiling water. Wool cannot be boiled without shrinking into a clotted, shapeless mass. Before cotton, you were sewn into your woolen underwear for the winter and often your body became a nesting ground for lice and disease" (374). While showing signs of the popular orientation of the book, these facts do not lessen the impressiveness of the scholarship which has gone into it.

One critic feels that "As a work of historical writing, *Wanderings* is a mixed performance. Mr. Potok can produce a good, strong narrative that also maintains a sense of historical proportion; and his occasional evocations of settings and feelings do contribute to a fuller sense of the past. But often the pursuit of drama gets him into trouble and the writing becomes stylized. . . ."[11] I do not agree with the judgment that the writing becomes stylized. In fact, Potok's skill as a novelist gives him the ability to use a variety of styles, thus avoiding an adherence to a conventional or single one.

In addition to the examples already given, a striking instance of the multiplicity of stylistic approaches can be seen in Potok's depiction of Moses's reluctance to follow God's command that he take on the leadership of the Israelites and lead them out of Egyptian slavery. Potok writes that the literary form in which the Bible presents this situation "moves the dialogue into the bargaining arena of an oriental bazaar. God promises 'various wonders.' Moses is skeptical. God produces proof. Moses pleads poverty of speech. God becomes angry. Aaron, brother of Moses, will do the talking. Moses reluctantly accepts the call . . ." (66). The short sentences, which shift from Moses to God and back again, create a seesaw movement that mimics two parties engaged in bargaining. In fact, as Si Wakesberg comments, "Potok's prose mixes the old and new with great facility."[12]

Some criticism can be leveled at Potok for devoting less than forty pages out of the 398 of the text to the post-1700 period. His treatment of such major issues as the effects of the Enlightenment, the birth and growth of Zionism, the mass migration of Jews from Russia and Eastern Europe, the Holocaust, and the rebirth of Israel as a Jewish state are crammed into too limited a space. While he does succeed in making many sound observations, including some that startle by their frankness (in referring to the large number of German-Jewish converts to Christianity in the eighteenth century, he writes: "Their descendents, great-grandchildren of their children, may have fought in the armies of Hitler" [371]; and in referring to Israel: "all the wars have cost us less than three days at Auschwitz" [398]), this crucially important period in Jewish history demands more extensive treatment than Potok gives it.

Other treatments of Jewish history which have aimed at a popular audience have approached the problem somewhat differently. Abba Eban's My People: The Story of the Jews has a similar format to Potok's book in that it uses a large "coffee table" format with many photographs and heavy, quality paper. Of the 522 pages of the text, around 275 are devoted to the post-1700 period. While there is no bibliography such as Potok provides, the approach is scholarly, the prose straightforward and unmetaphorical with no vivid contrasts. Max Dimont's Jews, God and History does not use oversize pages and provides no photographs. There is a good bibliography. The "popular" aspect of the book lies in the racy, highly metaphoric style, with an interesting and somewhat idiosyncratic set of chronologies headed, "Here's When it Happened" preceding each main section.

Dimont devotes about 130 pages out of 417 to the post-1700 period, and combines the scholarly and popular in an interesting and offbeat manner. Both authors treat the modern period much more thoroughly than does Potok, perhaps because of his rabbinical training and greater knowledge and interest in the ancient world and biblical period.

Both Eban and Dimont present workable, effective syntheses of the scholarly and popular. Potok, also, succeeds in depicting the saga of Jewish history in a most readable form while still taking scholarly demands most seriously. He presents the Jews as a people who have preserved their identity while being forced into a wandering way of life. Desirous of the stability of a permanent geographical homeland, they are seen to have made the best of frequently intolerable circumstances by responding positively to particular elements in the majority culture and in their situations. The result has been a change, and sometimes a strengthening, of Judaism but never its demise. As Potok has said, *Wanderings* was needed to prepare him for *The Book of Lights,* his fifth novel. By clarifying what the "culture package" of Judaism consisted of, *Wanderings* enabled him to approach the world of Asiatic paganism, thus breaking new ground as a novelist.

Chapter Seven
The Book of Lights
The Kabbalah and Jewish Tradition

The Book of Lights takes Potok into new and exciting territory. A central issue involves the relatively little known area of Jewish mysticism, its respectability as a field of study and, more importantly, as a method of understanding the world. Gershon Loran, the protagonist, has had what he is convinced is a vision on a Brooklyn rooftop. This event has affected the future course of his life in that while he remains adrift, without solid spiritual moorings, he is waiting for a return and clarification of the vision in the hope that it will provide him with an insight into the cosmos that will explain his and mankind's relationship to God and God's to man.

Into this inner waiting and expectancy intrudes the moral issue of the extent of Jewish culpability for the development of the Atom Bomb. Gershon's best friend, Arthur Leiden, cannot live with the fact that his father, along with many other Jewish physicists, has been instrumental in developing the bomb. He has dropped his study of physics for that of Judaism. As rabbis and army chaplains, both Gershon and Arthur find themselves in Korea, with Arthur pressuring Gershon to visit Japan so that he can make some attempt at understanding and atonement. The dichotomy between the "light" of mysticism and the "death light" of the bomb becomes a central image in the novel.

Gershon must come to grips with an Asiatic world which has great beauty and has endured great suffering. It is a world having no knowledge of Judaism, but which makes it possible for him partially to understand more deeply the religious problems with which he is struggling. His experiences in Asia enable him finally to decide what to do with his life—study Kabbalah and mysticism. Max Dimont explains what the decision involves: "According to the Kabbalists, the Kabbala was given simultaneously with the Torah; but whereas the Torah was given to all, the Kabbala was revealed only to a few select saints, who, according to tradition, handed it down to a very small group of mystics. Throughout the centuries, this current of mysticism ran alongside Torah and Talmud, but always underneath their majestic achievements. It was regarded by its devotees as a second Oral Law, claiming authority from Scripture."[1]

Despite the esoteric nature of the Kabbalah, it had a profound effect upon the development of Judaism. Potok has said that mysticism "has a history that goes back certainly to the rabbinic period, possibly a little bit before that. Possibly originating with either Ezekiel or Daniel, or with some of the—as we might call it—cults of the rabbinic period, the early rabbinic period. But certainly there's mysticism in the Talmud. And it is clear that it was not an isolated phenomenon, in the Talmudic period. Some of the greatest rabbis simply took it for granted that one could make actual ascents, A-S-C-E-N-T-S, to God, through a variety of heavens. . . ."[2]

In *The Book of Lights* there is an ongoing argument concerning the value of concentrated study of the Kabbalah instead of the Talmud. Gershon Loran's Talmud teacher, Professor Malkuson, tells him: "Much better you should study Talmud. This is such foolishness. You wish to become a scholar of foolishness?"[3] Malkuson considers the Talmud directly relevant to the daily life of the Jew, its study an art form. Professor Keter, Gershon's Kabbalah teacher, takes a very different viewpoint regarding the value of the Kabbalah, which is to him "neither nonsense nor untouchable. Yes. It is the heart of Judaism, the soul, the core. Talmud tells us how the Jew acts; Kabbalah tells us how Judaism feels, how it sees the world. We are Western secular beings today, rational, logical, yes, and so we are embarrassed by Kabbalah, which is so irrational, illogical. But the tradition was not embarrassed: for nearly two thousand years it was not embarrassed. Great Talmudists were also great Kabbalists" (22). His stress is upon preserving something that has occupied the Jewish mind for at least two millenia. He does not even ask his students to believe in it; he wants them to preserve it for study as a central aspect of Jewish religious history.

Around 1300, Moses de Leon of Granada assembled from various sources a book called the *Zohar* (Splendour). This book encapsulated Jewish mystical thinking through the centuries and "captured Jewish minds and hearts and became after the Bible and the Talmud the third sacred source of Jewish inspiration and guidance."[4] This guidance was particularly needed after the Jews were forced to leave Spain in 1492, ending a residence that had included a golden age

of 400 years when the country had been under Moorish rule. The
expulsion had been such a horrendous event that meanings in addition to those given in the Bible and Talmud were sought in
explanation. Isadore Epstein observes that the exiles found great
strength in the *Zohar,* and "through its teachings they learned to
perceive in their own tragedies a reflection of the cosmic tragedy in
which God Himself, so to speak, was involved, leaving them thus
in no doubt as to the ultimate issue, and at the same time to
apprehend the spiritual agencies they had at their command for
resolving the tragedy, and securing healing and blessing both for
themselves and the world."[5]

In Safed, in the mountains of northern Israel, there gathered a
small group of Kabbalists under the direction of Rabbi Isaac Luria.
Safed had long been a center for mystical studies, and the group
gathered around Luria about the middle of the sixteenth century,
a generation after the expulsion from Spain, attempted to respond
to the catastrophe by developing a new understanding of Kabbalistic
lore. Gershom Scholem points out that "It may indeed be said that
with Isaac Luria a new period of Kabbalistic speculation was in-
augurated which must be distinguished from earlier Kabbalah in
all respects."[6] Although Luria retained certain doctrines found in
the *Zohar,* he expanded others and interpreted many in a different
manner. The important point is that "Lurianic Kabbalah . . . in
the main dominated Kabbalistic thinking since the 17th century
until recent times."[7] Another writer on the subject has observed
that "one cannot escape being struck by the scope of Luria's vision.
This Kabbalism is the most exciting of the many systems."[8]

Lurianic Kabbalism states that in order for the universe to come
into being, God had to "contract" his presence, which had filled
all space. This concept, though not entirely new, had not appeared
in the *Zohar.* It must also be stressed that when one refers to "God"
here, it is to the *En-Sof.* In the Kabbalah this "stands above the
creator God of the Old Testament. The *En-Sof* is 'nothing' &, if,
as the Old Testament has it, He created things in His own image,
He would create nothing. The only activity, if we could call it that,
of the *En-Sof* was the emanation of a ray of light. Nothing more."[9]
This incomprehensible non-Being produced a beam of light that
pierced the space which had been created by His contraction; it was
in that space, because of the presence of that light, that creation
occurred.

Creation took the form of "primordial man" (Adam Kadmon), from whose eyes, ears, nose, and mouth there emanated beams of light which were the *Sefiroth;* ten in number, they are the "internal psychic organs of God . . . understood as abstract entities through which all change in the universe takes place."[10] The *Sefirot* were to be gathered into "vessels." However, some of these were not able to withstand the force of the light entering them and broke. In the novel, Jakob Keter refers to this as a time when "even God lost control . . ." (229). This is the second element central to Luria's system and is called the "breaking of the vessels." The result of this catastrophe was chaos. The light of the *En-Sof* did not spread throughout the world and, as Gershom Scholem states, most of the light was "hurled down with the vessels themselves, and from their shards the *Kelippot,* the dark forces of the *sitra ahra,* took on substance. These shards are also the source of gross matter. The irresistable pressure of the light in the vessels also caused every rank of world to descend from the place that had been assigned to it. The entire world process as we now know it, therefore, is at variance with its originally intended order and position. Nothing, neither the lights nor the vessels, remained in its proper place. . . ."[11]

The "breaking of the vessels" caused evil to come into the world, a world which should have been perfect, illuminated by Divine light. Good and evil became mixed, intertwined, so that each attribute contained aspects of the other. This idea was related to the fall of Adam, which could not be avoided given that his ontological spiritual counterpart, the Adam Kadmon, had already experienced a "cosmic fall." Luria believed that all future human souls existed in Adam, so that when he sinned all mankind to be was similarly besmirched. What, then, could be done to return mankind unsullied to Divine grace? This question was answered by the third aspect of Lurianic Kabbalism, the "restoration" or "reintegration."

This "restoration" depends upon man himself. Although mankind possesses a soul that shares in the evil of Adam's sin, man has free will; that is, he can choose good over evil. The Jewish people have a particular role among mankind in this attempt at making mortal men divine once again. The exile of the Israelites was designed not primarily as a punishment but to spread the Jewish people over the world so that they could engage in carrying out a particular task: that of creating the conditions whereby the redemption, the arrival of the Messiah, could occur. When enough of the scattered sparks

of light from the broken vessels had been gathered up, when the
good had been separated from the evil, the Messiah had to come.
This ingathering of the dispersed light could be accomplished only
through prayer and following the commandments of the Torah. It
would achieve redemption not only for the Jewish people but for
all mankind. This is the reason for the creation of man and why he
finds himself among the shards of the vessels that compose this
world. Thus, it is man's destiny to complete a creation that was
imperfect from the beginning because of the "breaking of the vessels"
and Adam's concomitant fall. As Poncé states: "The problem of
restoring the original unity no longer lay in the area of the Divine.
Man was now equally responsible for the work of restoration. . . .
Somewhere there is an Adam within each of us in need of restoration,
in exile from the Garden. The aim of Kabbalism is the restoration
of the divine man in the medium of mortal man."[12]

Potok observes that when the Kabbalists wrote of making ascents
to God through prayer, they were not dealing in metaphors but in
actualities.[13] Jacob Keter asks Gershon:

"The details of the upper world, the rivers of fire in front of the Chariot,
the bridges across the rivers, the seven palaces in the firmament, the angels
that throng the palaces, Ezekiel's account of the Chariot—all this is literal?"

"Yes," Gershon said. "Yes."

"You are right," Jacob Keter said "I believe so too. Though I cannot
fathom it." (92)

Potok discusses how the Jews turned to the Kabbalah to help
explain the horrors of the exile in Europe. The gathering of the
sacred sparks, their separation from the evil in which they were
encased, which could be seen as the world in which the Jews were
existing, this situation could be viewed in terms of a garden: "To
gather up the sparks and repair the damage was now the task of
the Jew. The exile was like an abandoned garden choked with weeds.
The people of Israel was to be the gardener."[14]

Gershon Loran is one such gardener although he is not sure what
he believes. The novel traces the increasing attraction of Kabbalistic
doctrines for him. Doubts always remain, the leap necessary for
complete belief in a mystical worldview being extremely difficult
to make because of the difficulty of fully understanding the pecul-
iarities of the Kabbalistic vision. The doctrine of the *Sefirot,* for

example, "the ten stages of emanation that are the manifestations of the sapphirelike pure radiance of God that make possible creation, generation, and decay. Were these emanations identical with God? Were they a radiation or an expansion of God's essence? Did the process occur in ordinary time or in non-temporal time?" (57). Gershon is never quite certain. Potok explains that he is attracted to Kabbalah

because all the other categories that he has used as a possible source for meaning in his life just don't seem to work for him anymore. This is a very battered young man. Every time something good happens to him it's wrenched out of his life. . . .

My feeling is that when normal systems no longer work effectively for a religious individual, that individual will resort often enough to the apocalyptic dimension of the religious experience, to the expectation that very quickly the horrors of the world must be resolved, and will be resolved by God. I think it is a fall-back system. [15]

Gershon Loran does use Kabbalah as a refuge in a violent and incomprehensible world. What leads him to it initially, however, is a vision he has on a Brooklyn rooftop. This vision and the many he continues to have plays a central role in his develoment.

Visions and the Orient

Gershon Loran is a man adrift in a world which for him is without apparent meaning. He lives with his aunt and uncle in a "sunless" apartment, in a house in which "something had gone awry from the very beginning" (3). The basic structure of the house is flawed (heating, wiring, plumbing, the roof), bringing to mind the basic flaw in the universe as seen by some of the Kabbalists. Not only does the house have "something wrong with it, . . ." the neighborhood itself shows "a twisting river of random events: parents died in slow or sudden ways, children were killed, relatives slipped young from life" (5). Indeed, Gershon's own parents died when he was eight, and the cousin whom he loved was killed in World War II. He comes to feel the world to be a terrifying place in which things are always "breaking down." His name, Loran, is an anagram for a device of the same name and stands for "Long Range Navigation." It was invented in 1940 to help ships and airplanes discover their position. The system makes use of two radio stations called "master" and "slave" stations that transmit signals picked up by a receiver. The signals can be used to plot a position. The relevance to Gershon's situation is obvious, particularly as he is most directly influenced by two teachers—Jakob Keter and Nathan Malkuson.

Potok has chosen the names of these teachers with care: they represent the first and last (tenth) *Sefirah*, which are called *Kether* (Crown) and *Malkuth* (Kingdom). *Kether* contains the design of the universe, "the first expression of God's primal will, a will to will, an impulse & nothing more as yet."[16] *Kether* is presented as masculine and can be referred to as the King, having some of the qualities of the *En-Sof*. It is the creator referred to in the Book of Genesis but not the *En-Sof* itself. It is knowledge and thought and "contains all which will eventually flow forth from it."[17] *Malkuth* is the feminine harmonious principle: passive, "the slumbering world of our passions."[18] The Kabbalists believed that God was androgynous and was not complete in His present form; He required the exiled feminine element for completeness, as does man made in His image. Thus God, man, and the world would reach a state of harmony when *Kether* and *Malkuth* achieved union. The *Shekhinah*, God's feminine opposite residing in the *Sefirah Malkuth*, would add the passions to the thought of *Kether* to complete the creation.

This necessarily brief description of extremely complex Kabbalistic ideas does give, nonetheless, some sense of the interplay between the ideas of Gershon Loran's two teachers. His preference for the views of Jakob Keter are supported by the almost supreme position of the *Sefirah Kether*. The terms used to describe it—"King," "creation," "knowledge"—and the quality of containing "all which will eventually flow forth from it" gives it, and the teacher with whose name it is associated, great stature. Nathan Malkuson's Talmudic commitment to rationality and intellectuality does not appear to fit in with the feminine "passive passions" of the *Sefirah Malkuth*. However, this *Sefirah* represents the created world and the harmony of all the *Sefiroth*. Malkuson's orientation is toward this world as presented in the Talmud, and he dislikes the illogical and irrational world of the Kabbalah. One might even say that Gershon comes to view his adherence solely to Talmudic precepts as essentially "passive," the active course being the attempt to go beyond the Talmud through Kabbalistic study. As throughout the novel Gershon has visions of these two men, each expressing his own viewpoint, it is important to recognize their symbolic importance in terms of opposite *Sefiroth* which are, however, in need of synthesis.

The experience that sets Gershon on his life's path occurs unexpectedly although he desperately needs to find some meaning in his life and is, one might say, receptive to whatever insights may be offered. Going up to the roof of his Brooklyn tenement one night, he sees—or thinks he sees—a bitch whelping her pups. This creation of life on the filthy wet roof inspires in him a sense of wonder at creation, at the mystery of a universe in which such beauty can be created surrounded by the dross of the world. He wants to "caress something," but the bitch snarls at him, so he turns his attention upward: "Instead he reached up and brushed his hand across the sky and felt, actually felt, the achingly exquisitely cool dry velvet touch of starry heaven upon his fingers" (6). This refocussing of attention from earth to the heavens does not mean that he cuts himself off from earthly concerns. However, it does mark a turning point in his life in that he begins to try to understand earthly events in "heavenly," and increasingly kabbalistic, terms.

This experience may well have been a vision, for Gershon points out that the next morning the bitch and pups are gone, and no one knows anything about them. Later in his life he recalls the experience as an exchange of touches; he feels that he had touched the sky, and says to Arthur Leiden: "I felt something touch me. Oh yes, something touched me. I've been waiting to feel that touch again. Is that childish of me?" (292). Potok has said that "the book is the record of his waiting for that moment, and what he goes through as he waits."[19] The significance of that moment was that it gave him a sign that all was not chaos, that at its heart the universe is significant and meaningful.

Although previous to this event Gershon had had visions of his dead cousin, his life of visions really begins with this rooftop epiphany. Asher Lev saw the world differently from others; Gershon Loran does as well. Karen tells him, "Your eyes go somewhere else" (33), and we are told that "something seemed to be wrong with his eyes, a lack of focus, a strange glaze, a haunting softness" (56). He feels presences, senses things behind him, and occasionally feels "disembodied." His inner struggle to reconcile the world of negative material reality with the hopefulness perceived in his rooftop vision objectifies itself in an ongoing series of visions comprising his two seminary teachers, Nathan Malkuson and Jakob Keter.

In his support of the Talmud to the complete exclusion of the Kabbalah, Nathan Malkuson shows his commitment to the material reality of the everyday world. The Talmud, as Keter puts it, "tells us how the Jew acts . . ."; that is, it has a strong practical leaning. Gershon's visions often set Keter against Malkuson and reflect his own inner turmoil as to which way to lean himself. While still residing in the seminary, Gershon has a vision of the two teachers meeting and discussing the central issue which divides them and with which he is concerned himself. We are told that Gershon "fell into a dreamlike vision. He could feel the quiet as he moved in his vision through the dimly lighted corridors. Soon Professor Malkuson would emerge from his study" (25). He imagines Malkuson walking down the corridors and meeting Keter outside:

. . . I am a threat to you, my friend, am I not. You would like our world to be smooth and rational, would you not. You do not care to know of the rabbis, the great ones, who were filled with poetry and contradictions. There is deep, deep within us the irrational as well. It is our motor energy, our creative demon. You think we know the world only on the basis of what we observe or can deduce logically? As you grew up, did you meet no one who spoke of his experiences through the use of images rather than logic, who spoke of things that did not correspond to any reality we can observe? The irrational completes us.

You exaggerate, Keter, came the murmured reply. You have taken a tiny tributary and made of it a mighty river.

Ah, this is no tributary, my good friend. This is the soul of the matter, the soul, the life's breath. You know it in your bones and will not admit it.

You exaggerate, you exaggerate. You deceive the unwary with your exaggerations. (25–26)

Gershon then imagines them making a wager as to which of them will win him over to his viewpoint.

Despite Keter's stress upon the irrational here, he is highly intellectual and academic, pursuing his Kabbalistic studies through comparison and analysis of manuscript sources and linguistics. It is his respect for the irrational and the metaphorical that sets him apart from Malkuson. Keter can fully appreciate Gershon's *succah*, roofed with a camouflage net instead of with branches; he sees it having a "special beauty," one that "conceals and reveals simultaneously. It hides the sun and lets in the sun simultaneously." To

Malkuson, it is "not exactly a proper succah . . ." (199). Malkuson's reliance upon the strict letter of the Law prevents him from fully appreciating what Gershon has managed to do under the difficult circumstances of Korea, even though he can add, "But all things considered—." This is how Gershon envisions them reacting, and it tells us as much about his orientation as it does about that of his teachers. His visions are methods of considering divergent approaches to the Torah as well as devices through which his own subconscious predilections manifest themselves. To use Malkuson's term, Gershon has *éntheos* for Kabbalah because, like Jakob Keter, he finds the intellect insufficient on its own to fulfill his religious longings. The attraction he feels toward the immaterial and abstract in the Jewish tradition provides for him, as it does for Keter, a more valid path to the religious experience than does the rational alone. His personality and life experiences have determined the direction in which he must go and the form his visions take.

Gershon's visions are not restricted to his teachers; he has visions of what he thinks is God entering the *succah* and of the Angel of Death descending upon him in the library. On a number of occasions, birds appear to take on a special significance as though they are halfway between the earthly world and another world. While sitting beside the Hudson River with Jakob Keter discussing Kabbalah as part of his examination, Gershon finds himself aware of the presence of birds, real or imaginary. They seem to be carrying his thoughts or, perhaps, to be messengers. At one point he relates the birds to the "Jewish mythic consciousness." He conceives of it "charged, volatile, explosive, soaring in the imagination free and away from the yoke and discipline of the Law and the Covenant or using it as a path toward the deepest meanings of the Torah and the Commandments . . ." (93–94). He continues answering Jakob Keter's questions but is only partially there: "he was watching the white bird hover low above the water, wings stiff and still. And, slowly, it dulled and faded and winked out and was gone. He felt a moment of deep aching sadness and the swift surging beat of his heart. His eyes hurt" (95). Whether the bird is actually there is debatable. What is important is that Gershon uses aspects of the material world, be they actual, creations of his psyche, or emanations from above to lift himself into another, nonmaterial, realm. This is different from the insights into nature of, for example, the American Transcendentalists in that nature is more than symbol: Gershon may well be creating his own natural objects which he then proceeds to see in abstract terms.

Gershon has no control over these visions; indeed, he is often terrified by the presences which he senses. He is attempting to find whether there is a core of meaning in the universe, this concern being heightened by his experiences in Korea and the Far East. In one vision, Malkuson warns him against the lure of a beautiful pagan culture; however, Keter supports his quest, saying in Gershon's vision that the core of things "is the only area worth tampering with, Malkuson. Everything else is the periphery" (250). Keter warns him that his trip to Hong Kong and Macao will be a "descent" which "may not only be difficult but also menacing" (267). He says that he may not go with him there, thus leaving Gershon to cope with his reactions on his own. He advises him that though the profane is separate from the holy, "the holy contains a particle of the left side" (316); that is, it is possible to gain increased understanding of that which is holy through some understanding of the profane, the pagan. Keter now revises his resistance to accompanying Gershon on his trip, this time to Hiroshima, where all Gershon's resources will be needed. He advises him to try to understand Hiroshima in the light of the truths of the Zohar. Thus Gershon prepares himself spiritually for his coming ordeal. Subconsciously, he wants Keter, his spiritual mentor and father figure, to "accompany" him into the dangerous world of Asiatic paganism. Like Asher Lev with his Mythic Ancestor, Gershon manages unconsciously to retain Keter's guidance in his unconventional approach to an understanding of Jewish tradition.

Gershon's experiences in the Orient create a conflict within him concerning paganism and its relation to Judaism which, in turn, increases the need for the visions which he has. He is startled by the realization that Judaism is unknown to half the world, yet that half has developed a rich culture not noticeably worse and in many ways more beautiful than that of the West. He wonders whether the God to whom he prays also listens to the prayers of the Shinto, Buddhist, or Confucian Japanese; if so, what does that say about the centrality of Western religions? He asks God about the apparently pointless suffering of the Koreans; no answer is forthcoming. One can see here Potok's own experiences of the Orient. During his service as an army chaplain in Korea, he found that "It was not the anguish of my own people that sundered me—that I had come to accept as part of our destiny—but the loveliness and suffering I saw in the lives of pagans. Jewish history began in a world of pagans; my own Judaism was transformed in another such world."[20]

Gershon wants to have a look "At this half of God's world" (275) because, as Potok himself had been, he finds that the beauty and suffering of the Orient dramatically affects his view of the certainties that he has brought with him. Ambiguity and a new set of responses to fundamental queries are what Gershon is left with. As one critic puts it: "Gershon begins to experience the spiritual fire he has been wanting . . . ; he approaches a transcendent apprehension of beauty and holiness previously denied to him. 'He was being taught the loveliness of God's world in a pagan land,' and this troubles him."[21]

Before this "spiritual fire" can be experienced, Gershon discovers that he cannot pray. Potok writes of experiencing this situation himself in Korea and of understanding the scene in *The Sun Also Rises* where Jake Barnes finds prayer difficult if not impossible as a result of his spiritual malaise and that of his times. Gershon muses: "You lingered over these words because their meaning was suddenly no longer so clear as you had once thought" (144). Even after his return from Korea, he seeks advice from Professor Malkuson who advises him to "Do what you are doing. Either it will return or it will not. Prayer is not the only commandment. The study of texts is also commanded" (364). Yet, Gershon can feel an "inarticulate stirring" in a pagan temple and finds himself uttering a blessing in the presence of wild nature and Mount Fuji. The Koreans also work against the effects of the horror of the war: "He came close to sensing a dignity and strength in the suffering people of the land" (203).

The result of his experience in the Far East is a changed view of the world. He conquers "something inside himself," a fear that the horrors of existence demonstrate that the world is without meaning. When he returns home, both Karen and Jakob Keter sense a change in him, and in a letter to his parents Arthur Leiden observes that Gershon "appears to have shed a chrysalis of some sort" (360). In order to understand precisely what has changed in him, what he has understood, we must now turn to Gershon's relationship with Arthur Leiden and the issues raised by the light of the atomic bomb.

Light: Spiritual and Scientific

As the title implies, the central symbol is that of light, references to which occur throughout the novel. Potok builds major conflicts however around the light provided by religious insights as compared to the darkness of the world. He focuses upon science in particular and views it as ambiguous, its light becoming "dark" through the development of the atomic bomb. Referring to Gershon being a student of mysticism, the atomic scientist Charles Leiden says to him: "We have a mutual interest in light then, don't we"; to which Arthur's mother responds, "Very different sorts of light" (67). Gershon's spiritual teacher, Jakob Keter, was also attached to science but decided to leave it when he had a vision that science in the twentieth century would lead to death: "And so I decided instead to explore the demonic that leads to life, rather than the demonic that leads to death. It seemed to me that nothing was more demonically creative in all of Jewish history than Kabbalah" (119). He tells Gershon that Jewish mystics were obsessed with light: "It is of course incorporeal substance; so they thought. Appropriate for God and emanations. Today we speak of waves and particles" (90).

The light provided by science is seen to be discredited because it has led to the creation of a weapon which J. Robert Oppenheimer called the "death light." Potok presents the search for light in this century as fraught with difficulties. For a character like Gershon Loran who we are told "hated the night and its dark visions! Light, he needed light" (187), mysticism is a method of approaching the horrors with which he is confronted. His friendship with Arthur Leiden (German for "to suffer" or "sorrows") heightens his awareness of the moral issues highlighted by the atomic age.

In Arthur one sees an example of skillful characterization. Sensitive like Gershon, he feels deeply about moral issues. However, whereas Gershon convincingly works through introspection, Arthur is passionate and emotional, driven to distraction by his father's role in creating the atomic bomb. Like Keter, he rejects physics for religion, and for much the same reason: "All I could see were dead birds over the surface of the whole planet. And birds with burnedout eyes" (290). He does not want to advance physics but to "affect people. What good is physics in the hands of a species that is still partly reptilian? We'll kill ourselves with all that physics. I left to go to the seminary" (291).

Unlike Gershon, Arthur is unable to use mysticism as a means of discovering possible meaning in his world. Despite his being a rabbi, religion provides no real answers for him. He tries to come to grips with the world through direct action: associating with Korean revolutionaries and making some form of atonement to the

Japanese for the sins he associates with his father. Whereas Gershon is kept awake battling with his "four-o'clock-in-the-morning questions," battles that will eventually lead him to a form of reconciliation with the world, Arthur's struggles cannot lead him to a similar position because he is unable to tolerate the existence of such an evil as the dropping of the atom bomb on human beings. This difference between the two characters exists partially because of their individual personalities and on account of their experiences with death. Gershon's parents and cousin died themselves; Arthur's father did not die but was responsible, in Arthur's mind, for the deaths of thousands of strangers. In addition, Arthur considers his father partly responsible for helping to bring into existence a weapon of the greatest immorality. He takes his father's "crime" upon his own shoulders as both an individual and a Jew.

Potok makes the assumption that the Jews were largely responsible for the creation of the atomic bomb. Many Jewish scientists left Germany before the implementation of the "Final Solution" and became refugees in America. Einstein sent a famous letter to President Roosevelt in 1939 suggesting that he contact the physicists working in the field of atomic research to assure that the United States build an atom bomb before Germany did. As it happened, Hitler rejected the project, probably because of the immense cost in both money and manpower required; the large number of Jewish physicists in this branch of science also played an important part in his decision. Germany surrendered three months before the first bomb was dropped on Hiroshima, many of the scientists feeling that it had been dropped on the wrong enemy.

A number of critics have written that Potok erred in assigning such total "guilt" to the Jews. One commentator writes that "While Potok's anguish is understandable, his complete assignment of blame to the Jewish project physicists is inexplicable. He appears to ignore the fact that the bomb was an American project, for he leaves unimplicated in his righteous indignation the non-Jews who collaborated on the project, and most enigmatic is his failure to indict the politicians and military advisors whose decision it was to drop the bomb."[22] He has also been accused of taking "a peculiar relish in this drama of Jewish self-accusation and expiation."[23] In correspondence with Potok, I raised the issue of his reaction to this adverse criticism. He focused upon the particular question under discussion here:

The fact is that I did not invent that truth; I merely reported it. Theoretical physics is simply inconceivable in our country without Jews; indeed, in the early decades of this century physics was thought to be a particularly Jewish science. And theoretical physics, with the help of Szillard, Einstein, Teller, Oppenheimer, and other Jews, together with the organizational ability of American industry and the American military, made the bomb possible. It was to be a weapon against Hitler, whose scientists were thought at the time to be working hard at its development. Asking me to feel guilty as a Jew about that is like asking me to feel guilty as a member of humankind about the discovery of fire.[24]

Potok would have achieved a better balance of the facts if he had placed at least some weight upon the part played by non-Jews in the decision to drop the bomb twice on Japan. The closest he comes to this is in Charles Leiden's comment on the dropping of the bomb on Nagasaki ("We were in the hands of the witless" [360]), and in his rendition of Albert Einstein's commencement speech at the seminary when he says that he only wanted to understand the universe better, not make bombs. Speaking with regret of the letter he sent to President Roosevelt, we see the moral quandary in which he found himself; the situation seemed to justify his action. The graduation ceremony is punctuated by the sound of airplanes flying by, and Einstein's speech ends with a symbolic image: "An airliner flew by overhead. The sun had dipped behind the library building" (108). We are reminded of bomb-carrying planes, while the light of the sun recalls the light of the bombs; its disappearance behind the library has alternative implications of the darkness left after the bombs, the dimming of the light which shone upon the wisdom contained in the books in the seminary library. Also, one might say that this image implies the need to replace the light formerly seen in science with that contained in the theological texts housed in the library. In the atomic age religion offers the only light available.

Potok's presentation of Albert Einstein's attitudes parallels those he actually held. Reflecting his dischantment with his role in the development of the bomb, he said in 1945: "Since I do not foresee that atomic energy is to be a great boon for a long time, I have to say that for the present it is a menace."[25] The character Charles Leiden also expresses grave doubts as to his contributions as a physicist to the atom bomb project. After describing the Jewishness of the atomic physicists, he states that "we tinker with light and atomic bombs, with the energy of the universe. Do you wonder that the world doesn't know what to make of its Jews? No one is on more familiar terms with the heart of the insanity of the universe than is the Jew, and no one is more frenetic and untidy in the search for an answer" (234). His search led him to the Manhattan project, something he must now make his peace with, as must Einstein for his role in the atom bomb story.

Potok has said that all of his books came about "as a result of that moment in time when I stood in Hiroshima, trying to figure out where I was and what I was doing there, and what it all really meant to me."[26] Like Gershon and Arthur he stood before the monument, at the point where the bomb fell, and felt that the future of the human species had been irrevocably changed. Hiroshima is the place where Gershon receives a major jolt, which moves him closer to the time when he will have a final revealing vision. In the city Gershon feels that "Here a chasm has been opened to the empty future of the race. . . . All the darkness and light of the species were here in this city" (326). To Arthur, desperate to make some form of atonement, the city has the smell of death and "reminds you of the real possibility of an end to our species" (330).

A most striking use of light-dark imagery occurs in the horrific description of a picture postcard that Arthur cruelly chooses to send to his parents. It shows a gray stone stairway on which "The flash left the shadow of a man who was seated there at the moment. . . . A section of the stone was clearly darker than that all around it" (327). Charles Leiden will later tell Gershon that Arthur wrote on it, "Shadows on stones and shadows on lives" (360). The light of science has become a "death light." For both Gershon and Arthur the world has become a place where the best one can hope for is doubt and ambiguity. Gershon feels he can live with these better than with certainty, the light of Kabbalah providing at least a possible order and "balance to what he sees." For Arthur, however, this alternative is not possible: "All the world, it seems, is a grayish sea of ambiguity, and we must learn to navigate in it or be drowned. . . . What shall I do for my balance" (359).

Although Arthur's death would appear to end the need for his attainment of a "balance," Gershon still needs him, and he reappears in his vision in the final pages saying "Amen" to Gershon's recital of the *Kaddish,* the prayer for the dead and a statement of faith in God and His glory. This vision is somewhat opaque, the stress being

upon Gershon's descent deep into himself for answers rather than
his seeking an ascent to the "transcendent heaven." Before his Korean experiences and Arthur's death, he had felt that "If he were to
climb now, attempt the ascent, storm the palaces with all the things
he knew, he would perhaps see the Throne. Yes. And upon it would
be the Essence of all Being—encased in dark shrouds of melancholy.
He needed no such ascent. His small trench of earth was a parallel
sadness" (124). After his immersion in the loveliness and suffering
of the Far East, he cannot bring himself to flee from it and accept
what may be illusions. The result is that "all was now sealed to
him. He had not wanted it in the past, when it had been easily
accessible" (367). Note that even before his experiences in the Orient, he thought that the "Essence of all Being" would not be surrounded by light but "encased in dark shrouds of melancholy." His
early years have provided him with a notion of reality sufficiently
pessimistic to permit the possibility of his being able to come to
grips with the words from the "other side," "Is it that you are
surprised at the energies and insights possessed by the realms of
darkness?" (307).

He has decided to accept his own inner visions rather than those
emanating from "out there," until a different vision occurs. Arthur,
Gershon, and the "silken voice" all say "Amen" to the acceptance
of God's universe—its beauties and its horrors. The "other side"
becomes an acceptable part of Gershon's vision of reality, the "silken
voice" emanating from the darkness and telling him that "There is
some merit in darkness. There are times when light is a menacing
distraction. . . . There is already so much of me in your Kabbalah"
(308).

Gershon goes to Jerusalem to study with Jakob Keter to see
whether there is still any possibility of moving beyond the darkness.
He is not sure "Why one must do or say something" (369), but
though he now accepts the darkness he still yearns for the light. In
Keter's garden, "The air was shaded by tall trees, through which
streamed narrow pillars of light" (370). Light can come out of
darkness, but it can also be viewed as an entity with its own existence—the moral dimension or Godhead. We leave him waiting.

In this novel Potok returns to the pattern seen in *The Chosen* and
The Promise where two Jewish religious males from otherwise different backgrounds try to cope with some aspects of the modern
world. They are older in this novel and the issues are more complex,

but there are still teachers and authority figures, some of whom are positive and some not. This latter aspect also exists in *My Name Is Asher Lev* and *In the Beginning*. There is greater complexity here in that *both* men must make crucial adjustments of belief and attitude that do not fully solve their problems; their conflicts remain resistant to solutions with no neat endings being offered.

Potok has written that although he strives for a simplicity of style in all his novels, there are "some passages in *The Book of Lights* where deliberate ambiguity of style mirrors the subject of the book: ambiguity. . . ."[27] The novel has been criticized for being overly dull, gloomy, and lacking in dramatic effect. I think these criticisms unwarranted, and, indeed, many critical reactions have been positive, the reviewer in the *New Yorker* referring to the book as "A spare and graceful novel; the exotic setting makes Gershon an increasingly interesting character. . . ."[28] The ambiguity helps in making the characterizations convincing in that we see the two main characters involved in quests for meaning where a number of answers are possible and the full range of their personal needs is brought into play. Skill is required to present persuasively both the visionary and the perceived in Gershon's visions, the use of an omniscient narrator—not used in the other novels—giving the author a somewhat wider latitude than a first-person narrator would do.

For the first time, Potok comes to grips with sexuality in his characters. There was an awareness of sexual matters in *The Promise,* but this was limited both by the ages of the main characters and a certain priggishness due largely to their religious upbringing. In *The Book of Lights,* Gershon, who has also had a religious upbringing, sleeps with his fiancé, has sexual dreams about her, and is aware of the physical appeal of other women. Arthur occasionally swears, and four letter words appear in the description of Gershon's early exposure to street talk of sex and his reading of "porno books." The effect of Potok's treatment of these matters is to create in Gershon a believable, flesh and blood human being who yet possesses a strong moral code, as can be seen in his problematic treatment of Toshie. This is also reflected in Arthur's speech which, like Max Lurie's in the previous novel, readily presents his feelings without being filtered through an intellectual sieve. This frequently occurred in early novels where characters' emotions were held in check by virtue of their being raised in a culture that placed a premium upon intellectuality and held open expression of emotion—anger, distaste, etc.—in great suspicion. In this novel, Potok permits Arthur to overcome his staid New England, German-Jewish background and express himself forthrightly.

The Book of Lights shows Potok able to present a realistic rendition of places, areas of New York City and the Far East, using largely concrete diction; he has shown this talent in all of his novels. However, in this novel we see this skill counterpointed by movements into the abstract area of mysticism and visions, which require more connotative, metaphorical, and imagistic language. The tension created between the concrete and the abstract, and the ambiguities that occur because of this tension, has resulted in a satisfying and complex novel. Potok handles the complexities very well indeed. One feels that he has come of age as a novelist.

Chapter Eight
A Postscript on *Davita's Harp*

As this study was nearing completion, Chaim Potok's sixth novel appeared. This necessarily brief section is not intended as an exhaustive discussion of *Davita's Harp* but rather as an attempt to show its concerns, stylistic traits, and place within the Potok canon. For the first time Potok uses a female narrator, Ilana Davita recalling the events and impressions of her life between the ages of approximately eight to fourteen. The novel is set between 1936 and 1942 and is primarily concerned with a young girl's reactions to her own place in the world as a female, to the communism of her parents, the fight against fascism in the Spanish Civil War, and the problems raised by Orthodox Judaism in her life. Potok skillfully interrelates these issues so that one can see Ilana Davita Chandal's life as a battle to achieve a sense of selfhood, learn to cope with life's disasters, and develop an understanding of the religious and political forces which impinge upon her.

In all of Potok's novels, contemporary world events are important. Here, the depression and the rise of fascism in Europe contribute to the appeal of communism for Michael and Anne Chandal, Davita's parents. They wish to create a better world, but belief in their ideology is not shared by average Americans, and Davita remembers a string of forced changes of residence as her parents are ostracized by their neighbors for holding Party meetings in their various apartments. Also, she must cope with negative reactions at her school when her parents' political affiliations become known. To her mother and her father, who is killed in the Spanish Civil War, communism is a religion which they think is much more rooted in the real world than are traditional faiths. Potok clearly points out that like orthodox religious beliefs, communism requires discipline and an acceptance of doctrines that can blind its adherents to other possibilities. Because of her fervent belief in communist dogmas, Anne is spiritually destroyed when she hears of the Stalinist purges in Spain and the Nazi-Soviet Pact. Here, as in most of the previous novels, Orthodox Judaism can only provide a spiritual sanctuary for those willing to fit in, avoid certain questions, and not be overly individualistic. If Davita is to remain attached to Judaism, some other type or aspect must be considered, as indeed it is by many of Potok's rebels who would prefer to be Orthodox Jews if it were at all possible.

Potok is highly critical of Orthodox Judaism in this novel although he does, not entirely convincingly, manage to integrate Anne ("Channah") Chandal into the group. She has been presented as too much of a rebel and freethinker to be able to reverse her intellectual distaste for religion in general and to accept the decidedly second-class position of women in this group despite her earlier ties to Judaism in Europe. She like Davita cannot sit with men in the synagogue but must remain behind a curtain. Women are not supposed to say *Kaddish* (the prayer for the dead), and Davita receives strange looks when she insists on saying it for her father; Anne receives similar looks when she says it for Jakob Daw. Davita cannot be *bar mitzvahed*; and the Akiva Award, which she has earned, is withheld from her because girls cannot be seen to be capable of better academic performance than boys. Nonetheless, Potok ultimately presents this branch of Judaism as at least acceptable to Anne, although Davita decides to go to a public rather than to a Jewish high school as a reaction against negative experiences in her Jewish school. One has the feeling that she will move farther away from Orthodoxy than did Asher Lev, quite possibly leaving it entirely.

In addition to his treatment of Judaism, one should note Potok's positive presentation of Christianity through the person of Sarah Chandal, a deftly characterized nurse and Christian missionary. Aunt Sarah, as she is to Davita, is more admirable than either the believers in Orthodox Judaism or communism in that her religious beliefs have made her a selfless servant of those who suffer, be they members of her own family or strangers in foreign lands.

The range of religious belief or lack of it is greater in this novel than in any previous one. Michael Chandal dies rejecting his Christianity and trying to further the Communist cause in Spain. Interestingly, he perishes in Guernica while attempting to save a nun, his humanitarianism overriding political dogma. Davita will probably eschew Orthodox Judaism for a vision based closely upon that seen in the writer Jakob Daw's search for universal human truths. Daw has forsaken communism and is a reincarnation of the sculptor Jacob Kahn from *My Name Is Asher Lev*. Both artists live from deeply felt creeds that emanate largely from within themselves rather than being imposed from without, although Kahn makes it clear that art makes strong demands of its own. Both Sarah and Anne Chandal use religion as the basis for providing meaning to their lives. Anne is shown to develop religious belief slowly, and although she cannot yet pray the implication is that even this will come in time. This variation in the beliefs of the major characters is impressive, despite the proviso concerning Anne mentioned earlier. Potok had opted for complexity rather than simplicity, and this has made the novel richer and more convincing.

Stylistically, the novel shows some advances. Differentiation of speech patterns is more successful here than in previous novels. Through the use of diction, syntax, and choice of identifying phrases, Potok creates a number of characters who can be distinguished by the way in which they speak and not merely through their ideas and attitudes; Michael, Sarah, and Jakob Daw stand out in this respect. Unfortunately, there is the same flattening effect that one frequently found in a number of the previous novels to a greater or lesser extent. Not enough dramatic heightening of important moments occurs, although Potok does successfully provide the basis for the reader to empathize with a character's emotional state or situation.

Davita's first-person narration is largely effective in presenting the reactions and development of a young girl, a real achievement. Like all major juveniles in Potok's novels, Davita is extremely bright (her stepbrother is called a genius) and is capable of asking questions beyond the expectations of the adults. Frequently she does not understand the answers or appreciate the implications of them, but she is intelligent enough to be able to interest the reader in her inquiries. In part, she shows this intelligence through a suitably simple, given her age, level of biblical criticism. Potok clearly loves to have even a small amount of text criticism in his novels. A pupil named Reuven Malter is in her class, and he puts her straight as regards possible dangers in her interpretation of particular biblical passages. This is not a gratuitous intrusion but adds to her awareness of the basic rigidity of Orthodox Judaism, its fear of new ideas and approaches.

Potok presents the beginning of Davita's menstruation without quite enough stress upon the emotional upheaval which this physical change is likely to cause, although he does have her briefly hint at her awareness of the change in her life. Davita's emotions are given free rein in relation to her father, mother, and Jakob Daw. The death of the two beloved men cause her to suffer a movingly depicted nervous collapse. Her fantasies of them combine with the insecurity she feels when threatened with her mother's remarriage. Potok presents these emotional upheavals sympathetically and effectively.

While not reaching the standard attained in *My Name Is Asher Lev* and *The Book of Lights, Davita's Harp* is an impressive work. Potok has retained his by now expected use of school room situations, bright protagonists, controversy over Jewish religious dogmas, and concern with a particular historical period. However, he has chosen to require of himself new technical problems in each novel along with the presentation of new historical periods. In this novel, the historical events filtered through the mind of a young girl have made claims upon his skill not faced previously. While not being his best work, *Davita's Harp* is worthy of serious consideration.

Chapter Nine
The Writer Arrived
Jewish-American and American Literature

As do a number of other authors, including Saul Bellow and Bernard Malamud, Chaim Potok dislikes being labeled: "I do not care for pigeonholes like 'American Jewish writer' . . . unless one is prepared to call Cheever, say, an 'American Protestant writer.' I find distasteful the essentially reductionist label 'ethnic literature.' I am an American writer writing about a small and particular American world. Novelists, for the most part, deal with small and particular worlds. . . . I wrote about my small and particular New York world as Faulkner wrote about his small and particular Mississippi world and Joyce wrote about his small and particular Irish world. 'In the particular is contained the universal,' Joyce said."[1] He also feels that his world of Talmudic argument is as American as Faulkner's world of the Snopes because of America's great stress upon education and the value of scholarship.

Potok's point is well taken; his concern with the narrow world of Judaism still requires an astute understanding of the human condition and the ability to communicate it. The wide variety of backgrounds of his readers (all countries except the Soviet Union and China where his novels are banned, and probably more than half being non-Jews) shows that he is doing more than presenting an ethnic group, important and successful though this presentation is and colorful and exotic to a non-Jewish readership though it may be. He is showing how the universal can exist within the particular and how religious and cultural borders need not be barriers to understanding.

More particularly, one can see how Potok is a part of American literature. He presents numerous instances of clashes with authority figures—the classic father-son motif. One finds this in such American literary works as *Billy Budd, Sailor*, *The Adventures of Huckleberry Finn*, and *Death of a Salesman* among numerous others. Potok's fathers are never of the ilk of Pap Finn, are usually loving if not understanding, and are sometimes almost saintly (David Malter); nonetheless, they usually provide an important source of the conflict in the novels and, whether they are biological or symbolic fathers, frequently encapsulate attitudes from which the protagonist must flee.

Potok frequently "objectifies" his youthful protagonists' anguished detachment from the community in terms of their battles with their fathers, who individualize community values. Just as accommodation with the fathers' views becomes more difficult as one moves from novel to novel so does reintegration into the community, the protagonists having to depend upon sources—alive, dead, or visionary—outside it in order to fulfill themselves, justify their actions, and provide at least the possibility in most instances to remaining a part of some aspect of Judaism. Thus, Danny turns to David Malter; Asher to Jacob Kahn and to his mythic ancestor; David Lurie to his Uncle David; Gershon to the Silken Voice; and Davita to Jacob Daw.

Before any of Potok's novels were published, Robert Alter wrote that the Jewish character had gone beyond fitting in with American literary tradition and had actually supplanted the traditional American literary character: "From the larger American point of view, the general assent to the myth of the Jew reflects a decay of belief in the traditional American literary heroes—the eternal innocent, the tough guy, the man in quest of some romantic absolute—and a turning to the supposed aliens in our midst for an alternative image of the true American."[2] In fact with the exception of the "tough guy," Potok's characters have strong elements of Alter's other two types. His novels are bildungsroman (novel of formation) and *Kunstlerroman* (artist novel) in which the protagonists develop and grow in understanding, thus not remaining "eternal" innocents. However, even at the end of his novels, the protagonists could not be described as having totally lost their innocence and their quest for a "romantic absolute" remains.

Potok himself sees his work as within the American literary tradition. Responding to Sheldon Grebstein's comment that *The Chosen* is "middlebrow" because it permits "adjustment" on the part of the characters and high art never does, he writes that "It has been pointed out by John Clayton and others that alienation, dread, loneliness are basic elements in American literature from Irving and Cooper to the present; but so is affirmation of human potentialities, the worth of the individual, the return to Society. Huck Finn goes home; Hester Prynne's *A* ends up standing for "Angel"; Ishmael is healed, as are the heroes of *Invisible Man* and *Herzog*. American literature is not entirely a landscape of nightmare. . . . Trilling's notion that serious literature should assume an adversary position with regard to the prevailing culture is, I think, correct."[3] The "prevailing culture" in Potok's novels is largely ultra-Orthodox or Orthodox Judaism, broadening to include other areas in the last two; he consistently takes an adversarial position, though, of course, this is only one possible aspect of serious literature.

Despite his reluctance to accept the label of "American Jewish writer," it is impossible to avoid considering Potok's work in relation to this aspect of American literature because he has developed this subgrouping to such an extent. In 1967 he felt that a Jewish novelist was "someone who is hung up on his Jewishness, who wants to get away from it and cannot."[4] He saw most Jewish novelists dealing with Judaism in an entirely unsatisfactory manner. Almost twenty years later, this feeling is still present in that he is appalled that "Jewish writers of note will write about Judaism with the sort of heedless or nonexistent research they would never dream of bringing to their writings on the general culture. Laws and customs are incorrectly set down; family relationships are routinely oppressive; Hebrew expressions are misrepresented and misunderstood; texts are misquoted. The tradition they write about is peripheral to their cultural world. . . ."[5]

Being a rabbi makes Potok unique among important Jewish-American writers. His knowledge, love, and commitment to Judaism have meant that his writing enters deeply into the culture and presents it in all its complexity. He understands the differences that exist between the various sects and is aware of the arguments between and within them. No other Jewish-American writer has brought such a depth of Jewish knowledge to his work, thus moving the religion and culture from the periphery, where it exists in many novels, to the center. This attachment to Judaism has not prevented him from depicting its rigidities and intolerance and showing the desirability of particularly Orthodox Jews being more aware of what modern scholarship has to offer. He is also critical of the fear of individuality that religious fundamentalism inspires. Despite these criticisms, he sees Judaism, by implication of the non-Orthodox,

nonfundamentalist variety, as providing a panacea to the aimlessness
and anxiety that exists in the modern world.

Most Jewish-American writers show a qualified optimism in their
approach to the human situation. Potok does as well, his first two
novels leaning more toward almost complete optimism. Like Saul
Bellow, he has shown a faith in mankind, although his more recent
work has cast doubts on how much reliance one should place on
this particular faith. He believes that the universe is ultimately
meaningful and that mankind should engage in a search for meaning
in spite of signs of meaninglessness which may occur. He has written:
"I prefer to say, yes—now how do I cope with the meaninglessness?—rather than no—now how do I account for the meaningfulness?"[6] At heart, he remains an optimist, though one who
recognizes that there are no easy answers. One must make commitments, but he feels that "what you do is make your commitments
in the teeth of the ambiguity."[7]

Overviews

Potok has said that his novels up to *The Book of Lights* were inspired
by a need to come to grips with his experiences in Korea. He kept
trying to write a novel about what he had felt in Asia: "And every-
time I wrote it, I ended up back-flashing to the kid who went there,
and what I had to uncover was what it was that that boy was all
about."[8] The novels he wrote pitted "that boy" against the various
aspects of Western secular humanism which we have discussed in
the course of this study: Freudian psychoanalytic theory, scientific
text criticism, the aesthetics of Western art, and scientific Bible
scholarship which encapsulates aspects of Western anti-Semitism.
From a position at the center of their Jewish subculture, their
responses to Jewish Orthodoxy vary: "Danny Saunders says Yes.
Reuven Malter says Yes. Asher Lev says Perhaps. David Lurie says
No."[9] One could add that Gershon Loran and Davita Chandal also
say no. Although many of these characters reject the religious fundamentalism of their tradition, clearly they do not reject a religious,
a spiritual, approach to life. Potok does not think that "a tradition
that is static can be a viable tradition for any thinking individual
in the twentieth century."[10] A tradition that avoids coming to grips
with the problems thrown up by the secular world will, he thinks,
become stultified and barren.

Potok has said that he finds it difficult "to be fashionably comedic or ironic about the world. Nor have I been especially interested in mirror-games with words—unless I can use those games, as I do in the new novel *Davita's Harp*, for purposes beyond the game itself."[11] He thinks that his "heavy" yeshiva education, lasting around fifteen years, made a comedic approach to twentieth-century problems very difficult. It gave him "the heaviness of sanctity to fall back on, or the heaviness of mystery. There are no mysteries to the secular humanist," who frequently relies on humor to tackle "an essentially impossible world."[12]

A reliance upon irony frequently denotes a more pessimistic approach to characters than Potok is wont to take. With the possible exception of Davita, in his most recent novel, his main characters do not become alienated from or uncommitted to all aspects of Judaism. Potok is able to pursue his central theme of culture conflict without leaving his characters spiritually adrift. Gershon Loran, for instance, while left waiting is, nonetheless, sitting in Jakob Keter's garden having decided on a possible direction. Even Davita Chandal knows what she does not want and is leaning strongly toward the "spiritual" truths of literature. For her, Orthodox Judaism has failed to provide an acceptable resting place, but her alienation from it has been replaced by something that may help her come to grips with life's ambiguities.

Potok makes no apologies for his style, which has been the most consistently criticized aspect of his work. He has stated that "Each of the novels was rewritten four or five times from start to finish; sections of them were rewritten more than a dozen times. I work very hard to achieve that simplicity of style. There is a great deal concealed beneath that simplicity."[13] He feels that this spare style suits his characters and their situations, "Some narratives need to be lean, clean, and a touch bumpy."[14] He goes farther than this in thinking that language in "breathtaking arabesques" frequently hides a lack of depth.

We have seen the shortcomings of this approach in a number of his novels and the way in which he can fail to achieve the effects of this Hemingwayesque ideal. However, we have also seen how this style can be effective, particularly in *My Name Is Asher Lev* and *The Book of Lights*, his most successful works. Even in *The Promise*, his weakest novel stylistically, the ideas and conflicts retain one's interest. He is a traditionalist who, like Isaac Singer, believes in the importance of story and plot. While he says that he can appreciate avant-garde, often plotless, writing he soon forgets it and has no desire to write it because it does not affect his "essential being."

He has said that he hopes to write a novel about Jerusalem, that would begin with the 1973 Sinai War. He would also like to treat the Holocaust through, perhaps, Asher Lev going on his quest to find Jewish forms and an aesthetic motif which would enable him to treat the Holocaust through art. He may continue the story of Davita Chandal through the Holocaust but says that he has not tackled the subject "head-on yet because I feel thoroughly inadequate to the task."[15]

While his work has not reached the very highest level, there have been parts of individual works that have. He has shown the ability to create characters who remain with the reader long after the novel is closed, to tackle difficult issues and complex situations, and to illuminate previously untreated areas of Jewish life. He has extended the range of Jewish-American writing and using the depth of his knowledge of Judaism has made an important contribution to American literature. These are no mean achievements, and he is still writing.

Notes and References

Chapter One

1. "Culture Confrontation in Urban America: A Writer's Beginnings," in *Literature and the Urban Experience* (New Brunswick, 1981), 161.
2. "The State of Jewish Belief," *Commentary,* August 1966, 126.
3. Ibid.
4. Ibid., 125.
5. "Culture Confrontation," 167.
6. Ibid., 163
7. Ibid., 163–64.
8. "A Reply to a Semi-Sympathetic Critic," *Studies in American Jewish Literature* 2 (Spring 1976):32.
9. Personal communication from Chaim Potok, 1985.
10. Ibid.

Chapter Two

1. *The Chosen* (New York, 1967), 232; hereafter cited in the text.
2. Louis Jacobs, *Hasidic Prayer* (London: Routledge & Kegan Paul, 1972), 126–27.
3. Solomon Poll, *The Hasidic Community of Williamsburg* (New York, 1969), ix–x.
4. Ibid., ix.
5. Allen Guttman, *The Jewish Writer in America: Assimilation and the Crisis of Identity* (New York, 1971), 126.
6. Judah Stampfer, review of *The Chosen, Judaism,* Fall 1967, 495.
7. Ibid., 495–96.
8. Ibid., 497.
9. Hugh Nissenson, review of *The Chosen, New York Times Book Review,* 7 May 1967, 5.
10. Jacobs, *Hasidic Prayer, 14.*
11. Sam Blufarb, "The Head, the Heart and the Conflict of Generations in Chaim Potok's *The Chosen,*" *College Language Association Journal* 14 (June 1971):405.
12. Sheldon Grebstein, "The Phenomenon of the Really Jewish Best Seller: Potok's *The Chosen,*" *Studies in American Jewish Literature* 1 (Spring 1975):25.
13. David Daiches, "Breakthrough," in *Contemporary American-Jewish Literature: Critical Essays,* ed. Irving Malin (Bloomington, 1973), 31.

14. Loren Baritz, "A Jew's American Dilemma," *Commentary,* June 1962, 525.

15. Ibid.

16. "Reply to a Semi-Sympathetic Critic," 31.

17. Poll, *Hasidic Community,* 55.

18. "Reply to a Semi-Sympathetic Critic," 32–33.

19. Cheryl Forbes, "Judaism Under the Secular Umbrella," *Christianity Today* 22 (8 September 1978):20. Lillian Kremer states that "The elder Malter, patterned after the novelist's beloved father-in-law, Max Isaac Mosevitzky, is the idealized Jewish teacher, a dedicated scholar and humanitarian" ("Chaim Potok," in *Dictionary of Literary Biography* [Detroit, 1984], 28:234).

20. Poll, *Hasidic Community,* 61.

21. Bluefarb, "The Head, the Heart," 407.

22. Faye Leeper, "What is in the Name," *English Journal,* January 1970, 63.

23. Stampfer, review of *The Chosen,* 497.

24. Bernard Sherman, *The Invention of the Jew: Jewish-American Education Novels, 1916–1964* (New York: Thomas Yoseloff, 1969), 20.

25. Irving Malin, *Jews and Americans* (Carbondale: Southern Illinois University Press, 1966), 33.

26. Ibid., 32.

27. Bluefarb, "The Head, the Heart," 406.

28. Baruch Hochman, review of *The Chosen, Commentary,* September 1967, 108.

29. Grebstein, "Phenomenon of the Really Jewish Best Seller," 23.

30. Kay Dick, review of *The Chosen, Spectator,* 18 August 1967, 192.

31. Eliot Fremont-Smith, review of *The Chosen, New York Times,* 16 June 1967, 45.

32. Granville Hicks, review of *The Chosen, Saturday Review,* 29 April 1967, 26.

33. Daphne Merkin, "Why Potok is Popular," *Commentary* 61 (February 1976):74.

34. Marshall Breger and Bob Barnhart, "A Conversation with Isaac Bashevis Singer," in *Critical Views of Isaac Bashevis Singer,* ed. Irving Malin (New York: New York University Press, 1969), 35–36.

35. Grebstein, "Phenomenon of the Really Jewish Best Seller," 27.

36. "Reply to a Semi-Sympathetic Critic," 32.

37. Ibid.

Chapter Three

1. "The First Eighteen Years," *Studies in American Jewish Literature* 4 (1985):100–101. See also review of *The Promise, Time Magazine,* 12 September 1969, 78.

2. *The Promise* (New York, 1969), 291; hereafter cited in the text.

3. Lillian Elkin, review of *The Promise, Jewish Frontier,* March 1970, 25.

4. Ibid., 25–26.

5. "The State of Jewish Belief," 125.

6. "The Role of the Jewish Artist: As Jew, As Citizen, As Craftsman," *Congress Bi-Weekly,* 15 March 1974, 11.

7. *Encyclopedia Judaica,* s.v. "Luria, Solomon Ben Jehiel."

8. Ibid., s.v. "Pineles, Hirsch Mendel Ben Solomon."

9. Ibid., s.v. "Epstein, Jacob Nahum."

10. "Role of the Jewish Artist," 11.

11. "Interaction in the Adopted Land," *Saturday Review* 51 (7 December 1968):37.

12. Elkin, review of *The Promise,* 26.

13. Hugh Nissenson, review of *The Promise, New York Times Book Review,* 14 September 1969, 5.

14. Grebstein, "Phenomenon of the Really Jewish Best Seller," 28.

15. Dorothy Rabinowitz, review of *The Promise, Commentary,* May 1970, 106.

16. Personal communication from Chaim Potok, 1985.

17. Curt Leviant, review of *The Promise, Saturday Review,* 20 September 1969, 37.

18. James Joyce, *Ulysses* (New York: Vintage Books, 1966), 724.

19. James G. Murray, review of *The Promise, America,* 4 October 1969, 274.

20. Ibid.

21. Leviant, review of *The Promise,* 37.

22. Michael T. Gilmore, review of *The Promise, Midstream* 16 (January 1970):78.

23. Saul Bellow, "Where Do We Go From Here: The Future of Fiction," in *Saul Bellow and the Critics,* ed. Irving Malin (New York: New York University Press, 1969), 220.

24. Elkin, review of *The Promise,* 26.

Chapter Four

1 . Pat Pfeiffer, "The World of Chaim Potok," *Inside,* Winter 1981, 103 .

2. Forbes, "Judaism," 21.

3. "Role of the Jewish Artist," 4.

4. Ibid., 11.

5. Ibid., 5.

6. Ibid., 11.

7. *My Name Is Asher Lev* (New York, 1972), epigraph; hereafter cited in the text.

8. Elaine Lindsay, "Chaim Potok: Interview," *Literature in North Queensland* 6 (1978):69.

9. "Role of the Jewish Artist." 3.

10. Forbes, "Judaism," 20.

11. Lindsay, "Chaim Potok," 69–70.

12. Cecil Roth, introduction to *Jewish Art: An Illustrated History,* ed. Cecil Roth, revised by B. Narkiss (London: Valentine, Mitchell, 1971), 19.

13. J. H. Hertz, ed., *The Pentateuch and Haftorahs,* 2d ed. (London: Soncino Press, 1972), 295.

14. Roth, introduction, 11–12.

15. Warren True, "Potok and Joyce: the Artist and His Culture," *Studies in American Jewish Literature* 2 (1982):188.

16. Sam Sutherland, III, "Asher Lev's Vision of His Mythic Ancestor," *Re: Artes Liberales* 3 (1977):51.

17. Ibid., 53.

18. Ellen Uffen, "My Name is Asher Lev: Chaim Potok's Portrait of the Young Hasid as Artist," *Studies in American Jewish Literature* 2 (1982):174.

19. Sydney Feshbach sees three fathers in the novel: "a biological father (Aryeh Lev), artistic father (Kahn) and a religious father (the Rebbe). . . ." One could argue that Asher's resolution of his problem consists of an almost complete acceptance of the views of his artistic father but with a leavening from the views of his religious one. In this interpretation, his biological father's ideas are forsaken because of their rigidity ("Is That You, Chaim Potok?" *Studies in American Jewish Literature* 3 [Spring 1977]:36).

20. Uffen, "My Name is Asher Lev," 179.

21. S. Lillian Kremer, "Dedalus in Brooklyn: Influences of *A Portrait of the Artist as a Young Man* on *My Name Is Asher Lev,*" *Studies in American Jewish Literature* 4 (1985):26–38.

22. Review of *The Dean's December, Philadelphia* 73 (March 1982):72, 74.

23. T. Lask, review of *My Name Is Asher Lev, New York Times,* 21 April 1972, 37.

24. Ibid.

25. W. Speers, "Chaim Potok," *Philadelphia Inquirer,* 11 April 1983, 4c.

26. Forbes, "Judaism," 17.

27. Lindsay, "Chaim Potok," 69.

28. Edward G. Moore, "Why Potok Writes," *Literary Sketches* 16 (June 1976):2.

29. Sutherland, "Asher Lev's Vision," 52.

30. "Role of the Jewish Artist," 11.

31. Forbes, "Judaism," 16–17.

32. Review of *My Name Is Asher Lev*, *New Yorker*, 27 May 1972, 114.

33. Guy Davenport, review of *My Name Is Asher Lev*, *New York Times Book Review*, 16 April 1972, 18.

34. Speers, "Chaim Potok," 4c.

35. Ibid.

Chapter Five

1. *In the Beginning* (New York, 1975), 82; hereafter cited in the text.

2. "The State of Jewish Belief," 126.

3. Leonard Cheever, "Rectangles of Frozen Memory: Potok's *In the Beginning*," *Publications of the Arkansas Philological Association* 4 (1978):9.

4. Forbes, "Judaism," 20.

5. *Wanderings: Chaim Potok's History of the Jews* (New York, 1978), 390.

6. Kremer, "Chaim Potok," 239.

7. Hugh Nissenson, review of *In the Beginning*, *New York Times Book Review* 42 (19 October 1975):38.

8. Forbes, "Judaism," 20.

9. Ibid.

10. Ibid., 15.

11. Ken Shelton, "Writer on the Roof," *BYU Today*, April 1983, 11.

12. Forbes, "Judaism," 21.

13. It is noteworthy that Louis Jacobs no longer serves as a rabbi within official English Orthodoxy. He has become a rabbi who is independently Orthodox, which is close in beliefs and practices to American Conservatism—the group to which Chaim Potok belongs (see Potok's review of *Principles of the Jewish Faith*, *Commentary* 39 [May 1965]:78, 80).

14. Shelton, "Writer on the Roof," 11.

15. "State of Jewish Belief," 127.

16. Review of *In the Beginning*, *New Yorker*, 17 November 1975, 193.

17. Kremer, "Chaim Potok," 240.

Chapter Six

1. Pfeiffer, "World of Chaim Potok," 55.

2. *Wanderings: Chaim Potok's History of the Jews* (New York, 1978), 25–27; hereafter cited in the text.

148 CHAIM POTOK

3. "The Mourners of Yehezkel Kaufmann," *Conservative Judaism,* Winter 1964, 8–9.
4. Ibid., 9.
5. "When Culture Confronts Faith: An Interview with Chaim Potok," *College People* 3 (October 1983):11.
6. Robert Dahlin, "In His First Nonfiction, Potok Follows the Trails of the Jews Through History," *Publishers Weekly* 213 (22 May 1978):212.
7. Si Wakesberg, review of *Wanderings, Jewish Frontier,* May 1979, 26.
8. Alan Mintz, review of *Wanderings, New York Times Book Review,* 17 December 1978, 3.
9. "Heroes for an Ordinary World," in *The Hero and the Heroic Ideal: A Symposium* (Chicago, 1973), 76.
10. Wakesberg, review of *Wanderings,* 26.
11. Mintz, review of *Wanderings,* 34.
12. Wakesberg, review of *Wanderings,* 26.

Chapter Seven

1. Max Dimont, *Jews, God and History* (New York: New American Library, 1962), 267.
2. Martin Bookspan, "A Conversation with Chaim Potok," *The Eternal Light,* no. 1453, N.B.C. Radio Network, 22 November 1981 (New York: Jewish Theological Seminary of America, 1981), 2.
3. *The Book of Lights* (New York, 1981), 18; hereafter cited in the text.
4. Isadore Epstein, *Judaism* (Harmondsworth: Penguin Books, 1973), 243.
5. Ibid.
6. *Encyclopedia Judaica,* s.v. "Kabbalah."
7. Ibid.
8. Charles Poncé, *Kabbalah: An Introduction and Illumination for the World Today* (London: Garnstone Press, 1974), 83.
9. Ibid., 98.
10. Ibid., 101–3.
11. *Encyclopedia Judaica,* s.v. "Kabbalah."
12. Poncé, *Kabbalah,* 140.
13. Bookspan, "Conversation with Chaim Potok," 2.
14. *Wanderings,* 332.
15. "When Culture Confronts Faith," 10–11.
16. Poncé, *Kabbalah,* 115.
17. Ibid., 243.
18. Ibid., 154.

19. Bookspan, "Conversation with Chaim Potok," 7.

20. *Wanderings,* xiv.

21. Johanna Kaplan, review of *The Book of Lights, New York Times Book Review,* 11 October 1981, 15.

22. Kremer, "Chaim Potok," 241.

23. Ruth R. Wisse, "Jewish Dreams," *Commentary* 73 (March 1982):48.

24. Personal communication from Chaim Potok, 1985.

25. Albert Einstein, "Einstein on the Atomic Bomb," in *The 1940's: Profile of a Nation in Crisis,* ed. Chester Eisinger (New York: Anchor Books, 1969), 102.

26. Bookspan, "Conversation with Chaim Potok," 9.

27. Personal communication from Chaim Potok, 1985.

28. Review of *The Book of Lights, New Yorker,* 9 November 1981, 206.

Chapter Nine

1. "First Eighteen Years," 105–6.

2. Robert Alter, "Sentimentalizing the Jews," *After the Tradition: Essays on Modern Jewish Writing* (New York: E. P. Dutton & Co., 1971), 39.

3. "Reply to a Semi-Sympathetic Critic," 33–34. See also the quotation referred to in chapter 2, n. 12.

4. "Authors and Editors," *Publishers Weekly,* 3 April 1967, 25.

5. "First Eighteen Years," 104–5.

6. Speers, "Chaim Potok," 4c.

7. Ibid.

8. Bookspan, "Conversation with Chaim Potok," 8.

9. "Reply to a Semi-Sympathetic Critic," 33.

10. Bookspan, "Conversation with Chaim Potok," 9.

11. "First Eighteen Years," 105.

12. S. Lillian Kremer, "An Interview with Chaim Potok, July 21, 1981," *Studies in American Jewish Literature* 4 (1985):94.

13. Personal communication from Chaim Potok, 1985.

14. Ibid.

15. Alan Abrams, "When Cultures Collide," *Jewish News* (Detroit), 2 June 1984, 54.

Selected Bibliography

PRIMARY SOURCES

1. Novels
The Book of Lights. New York: Alfred A. Knopf, 1981.
The Chosen. New York: Simon & Schuster, 1967.
Davita's Harp. New York: Alfred A. Knopf, 1985.
In the Beginning. New York: Alfred A. Knopf, 1975.
My Name Is Asher Lev. New York: Alfred A. Knopf, 1972.
The Promise. New York: Alfred A. Knopf, 1969.

2. History
Wanderings: Chaim Potok's History of the Jews. New York: Alfred A. Knopf, 1978.

3. Uncollected Short Stories
"The Cats of 37 Alfasi Street." *American Judaism,* Fall 1966, 12–13, 25–29.
"The Dark Place Inside." *Dimensions,* Fall 1967, 35–39.
"The Fallen." *Hadassah Magazine,* December 1973, 6–7.
"The Gifts of Andrea." *Seventeen,* October 1982, 152–53, 168–71.
"Miracles for a Broken Planet." *McCall's,* December 1972, 36.
"Reflections on a Bronx Street." *Reconstructionist,* 2 October 1964, 13–20.
"A Tale of Two Soldiers." *Ladies' Home Journal,* December 1981, P.S. 16–19.

4. Pamphlet Collection
Ethical Living for a Modern World: Jewish Insights. New York: Jewish Theological Seminary of America, 1985.

5. Essays (arranged chronologically)
"The Mourners of Yehezkel Kaufmann." *Conservative Judaism,* Winter 1964, 1–9.
"The Naturalism of Sidney Hook." *Conservative Judaism,* Winter 1964, 40–52.
"Martin Buber and the Jews." *Commentary,* March 1966, 43–49.

"The State of Jewish Belief." *Commentary*, August 1966, 125–27.

"Letter." *Commentary*, September 1966, 24, 27, 28. Reply to comments on the "Martin Buber" article.

"Jews of the 1970's." *Ladies' Home Journal*, December 1969, 134.

"Heroes for an Ordinary World." In *The Hero and the Heroic Ideal: A Symposium*, 70–76. Chicago: Encyclopaedia Brittanica, 1973.

"Foreword." *Firstfruits: A Harvest of 25 Years*. Philadelphia: Jewish Publication Society of America, 1973.

"The Role of the Jewish Artist: As Jew, As Citizen, As Craftsman." *Congress Bi-Weekly*, 15 March 1974, 3–12.

"A Reply to a Semi-Sympathetic Critic." *Studies in American Jewish Literature*, Spring 1976, 30–34.

"Culture Confrontation in Urban America: A Writer's Beginnings." In *Literature and the Urban Experience*, edited by Michael Jaye and A. Watts, 161–67. New Brunswick: Rutgers University Press, 1981.

"What Will You Do When April Comes?" *Moment*, March 1982, 13–24.

"Teaching the Holocaust." *Philadelphia*, April 1982, 130–45.

"Barbra Streisand and Chaim Potok." *Esquire*, October 1982, 117–27.

"The Bible's Inspired Art." *New York Times Magazine*, 3 October 1982, 58–68.

"The Age of Permanent Apocalypse." *Pennsylvania Gazette*, June 1983, 39–41.

"Uncommon Philadelphia." *Goodlife*, August 1984, 18–25.

6. Reviews (arranged chronologically)

Review of *Martin Buber*, by Arthur A. Cohen. *Conservative Judaism*, Spring 1959, 50–52.

"Provisional Absolutes." Review of *Principles of the Jewish Faith*, by Louis Jacobs. *Commentary*, May 1965, 76–80.

"Letter." *Commentary*, September 1965, 22–24. Reply to comments on the review of *Principles of the Jewish Faith*.

"Interaction in the Adopted Land." Review of *The Joys of Yiddish*, by Leo Rosten; *Strangers and Natives*, by Judd L. Teller; *The American Jews*, by James Yaffe; and *Jewish Americans*, by Sidney Goldstein and C. Goldscheider. *Saturday Review*, 7 December 1968, 37–40.

"A Tale of Two Cities." Review of *The Dean's December*, by Saul Bellow. *Philadelphia*, March 1982, 71–74, 162.

"Stories from Bellow's Own Pungent Province." Review of *Him with His Foot in His Mouth and Other Stories*, by Saul Bellow. *Philadelphia Inquirer*, 20 May 1984, 1, 8.

"A Sorrowful Record of Ghetto Life." Review of *The Chronicle of the Lodz Ghetto, 1941–1944*, edited by L. Dobroszycki. *Philadelphia Inquirer*, 30 September 1984, 3.

"A Writer's Roots: Singer as Storyteller and as Young Artist." Review of *Love and Exile* and *Stories for Children*, by Isaac Bashevis Singer. *Philadelphia Inquirer*, 11 November 1984, 6.
"A Chilling Vision of a Nightmare World." Review of *The Burn*, by Vassily Aksyonov. *Philadelphia Inquirer*, 9 December 1984, 1, 6.
"The Exodus Story: Yet Another Meaning." Review of *Exodus and Revolution*, by Michael Walzer. *Philadelphia Inquirer*, 21 April 1985, 1, 6.
"Nathan Zuckerman's 'Dark and Terrible Pain.' " Review of *Zuckerman Bound: A Trilogy and Epilogue*, by Philip Roth. *Newsday*, 23 June 1985, 16, 13.

SECONDARY SOURCES

Abrams, Alan. "When Cultures Collide." *Jewish News* (Detroit), 22 June 1984, 13ff. A useful interview that includes Potok's views on the film of *The Chosen*, writing about the Holocaust, and future projects.
Bookspan, Martin. "A Conversation with Chaim Potok." *The Eternal Light*, no. 1453. Transcript of NBC Radio Network broadcast, 22 November 1981. New York: Jewish Theological Seminary of America, 1981. Potok discusses mysticism, Kabbalah, and *The Book of Lights*.
Bluefarb, Sam. "The Head, the Heart and the Conflict of Generations in Chaim Potok's *The Chosen*." *College Language Association Journal*, June 1971, 402–9. Article in which the themes of the title are interestingly pursued.
Cheever, Leonard. "Rectangles of Frozen Memory: Potok's *In the Beginning*." *Publications of the Arkansas Philological Association* 4 (1978):8–12. Article that analyzes the novel in terms of the photographs and books cited.
Dahlin, Robert. "In His First Nonfiction, Potok Follows the Trails of the Jews through History." *Publishers Weekly*, 22 May 1978, 212. Observations on *Wanderings* using many comments by Potok.
Davenport, Guy. "Collision with the Outside World." *New York Times Book Review*, 16 April 1972, 5, 18. Admiring review of *My Name Is Asher Lev* which also cites the two previous novels.
Elkin, Lillian. Review of *The Promise*. *Jewish Frontier*, March 1970, 25–26. Insightful discussion of the novel despite the misspelling of Potock's *(sic)* name.
Forbes, Cheryl. "Judaism under the Secular Umbrella." *Christianity Today*, 8 September 1978, 14–21. Useful wide-ranging interview in an evangelical magazine.

Gilmore, Michael. "A Fading Promise." *Midstream*, January 1970, 76–79. Analysis of *The Promise* in relation to some earlier Jewish-American novels and social history.

Grebstein, Sheldon. "The Phenomenon of the Really Jewish Best Seller: Potok's *The Chosen.*" *Studies in American Jewish Literature*, Spring 1975, 23–31. A good analysis of the novel, which includes discussions of style and the American Dream.

Guttman, Allen. *The Jewish Writer in America: Assimilation and the Crisis of Identity.* New York: Oxford University Press, 1971. Good general text on Jewish-American literature with an admiring short discussion of *The Chosen* and *The Promise.*

Hicks, Granville. "Good Fathers and Good Sons." *Saturday Review*, 29 April 1967, 25–26. Discussion of the father-son theme in *The Chosen.*

Kaplan, Johanna. "Two Ways of Life." *New York Times Book Review*, 11 October 1981, 14–15. Praises *The Book of Lights* for its treatment of difficult issues.

Kremer, Lillian. "Chaim Potok." In *Dictionary of Literary Biography*, edited by Daniel Walden, 28:232–43. Detroit: Gale, 1984. Thorough discussion of Potok and his work.

Leviant, Curt. "The Hasid as American Hero." *Midstream*, November 1967, 76–80. An analysis of *The Chosen* highly critical of its style.

Lindsay, Elaine. "Interview." *Literature in North Queensland* 6 (1978):68–70. Short interview focusing upon art in *My Name Is Asher Lev.*

Lipskar, Mendel. "My Name is Not Asher Lev." *Jewish Affairs* (South Africa) 32 (1977):31–32. Rabbi criticizes Potok's depiction of Hasidism in the first three novels.

Malin, Irving, ed. *Contemporary American-Jewish Literature: Critical Essays.* Bloomington: Indiana University Press, 1973. Useful collection of essays on Jewish-American literature.

Merkin, Daphne. "Why Potok is Popular." *Commentary*, February 1976, 73–75. Commenting on the first four novels but focusing on *In the Beginning*, the author analyzes Potok's appeal and is highly critical of his style.

Milch, Robert. Review of *My Name Is Asher Lev. Saturday Review*, 15 April 1972, 65–66. Praises the style of the novel and sees it as superior to the previous two.

Mintz, Alan. "A Series of Sojourns." *New York Times Book Review*, 17 December 1978, 3, 34. A discussion of *Wanderings* that praises its "dramatic immediacy" and historical research but criticizes its summaries of civilizations and "emphasis on cultural confrontation."

Nissenson, Hugh. "The Spark and the Shell." *New York Times Book Review*, 7 May 1967, 4–5, 34. An appreciative discussion of *The Chosen* stressing that the plot overcomes an unpolished style.

————. "The Jews Have Long Since Embarked." *New York Times Book Review*, 14 September 1969, 5, 21. *The Promise* is better than *The Chosen* but Potok is reluctant to dramatize.

————. "My Name is David Lurie." *New York Times Book Review*, 19 October 1975, 36–38. Admiring response to *In the Beginning*, a "powerful" novel.

Pfeiffer, Pat. "The World of Chaim Potok." *Inside*, Winter 1981, 54–55, 102–4. Good interview and commentary on Potok's ideas with stress upon *Wanderings* and *The Book of Lights*.

Poll, Solomon. *The Hasidic Community of Williamsburg*. New York: Schocken Books, 1969. Sociological treatment of this group, particularly relevant to *The Chosen*.

Rosenfeld, Alvin. "The Progress of the American Jewish Novel." *Contemporary Jewish Review* 7 (1973):115–30. Interesting article on the state of Jewish-American literature mostly since World War II in which Potok is seen as part of a new orientation to things Jewish.

Schiff, Ellen. "To Be Young, Gifted and Oppressed: The Plight of the Ethnic Artist." *Multi-Ethnic Literature of the United States* 6 (undated):73–80. Comparison of *Black Boy* and *My Name Is Asher Lev* as novels depicting examples of individuals suffering the intolerance of their own people.

Scholem, Gershom G. *On the Kabbalah and Its Symbolism*. Translated by Ralph Manheim. New York: Schocken Books, 1965. Useful text for aid in understanding the Kabbalah.

Shapiro, Karl. "The Necessary People." *Book Week*, 23 April 1967, 4, 12. Calling *The Chosen* an allegory, the poet responds positively to it.

Shelton, Ken. "Writer on the Roof." *BYU Today*, April 1983, 9–11. Interview with a Mormon periodical, which has a biographical slant.

Sherman, Bernard. Review of *The Chosen*. *Chicago Jewish Forum*, Spring 1968, 215–16. While critical of the novel's style, the author praises its plot and themes.

Speers, W. "Chaim Potok: He Quietly Built a Reputation; Now He is Going Public." *Philadelphia Inquirer*, 11 April 1983, 1c, 4c. Interesting interview touching on Potok's painting, background, doubts, and writing method.

Stampfer, Judah. "The Tension of Piety." *Judaism*, Fall 1967, 494–98. Stresses that *The Chosen* is truer to yeshiva than Hasidic life and is unsatisfactory in its presentation of Freudian psychology.

Stern, David. "Two Worlds." *Commentary*, October 1972, 102, 104. Not impressed with the first three novels, this reviewer of *My Name Is Asher Lev* is unconvinced of Asher's talent and Potok's skill.

Studies in American Jewish Literature 4 (1985). This issue entitled, "The World of Chaim Potok" is devoted entirely to his work and contains an interview and a range of essays, including one by Potok himself.

Sutherland, Sam, III. "Asher Lev's Vision of His Mythic Ancestor." *Re: Artes Liberales,* Spring 1977, 51–54. Analysis of the changing nature of Asher's dreams of his mythic ancestor.

True, Warren. "Potok and Joyce: the Artist and his Culture." *Studies in American Jewish Literature* 2 (1982):181–90. Comparison of *A Portrait of the Artist as a Young Man* and *My Name Is Asher Lev* in terms of the difficulties encountered by the two protagonists.

Uffen, Ellen. "*My Name Is Asher Lev:* Chaim Potok's Portrait of the Young Hasid as Artist." *Studies in American Jewish Literature* 2 (1982):174–80. Close analysis of the novel showing how Asher becomes part of both an alien and Jewish tradition.

Wakesberg, Si. "History as Narrative." *Jewish Frontier,* May 1979, 26. The author feels that *Wanderings* was written "with a novelist's craft and a poet's insight."

"When Culture Confronts Faith: An Interview with Chaim Potok." *College People,* October 1983, 8–13. Interview with a Seventh-day Adventist magazine stressing literary and religious issues.

Wisse, Ruth. "Jewish Dreams." *Commentary,* March 1982, 45–48. Unfair criticism of *The Book of Lights* in an article that also discusses S. Burnshaw's *The Refusers.*

Index